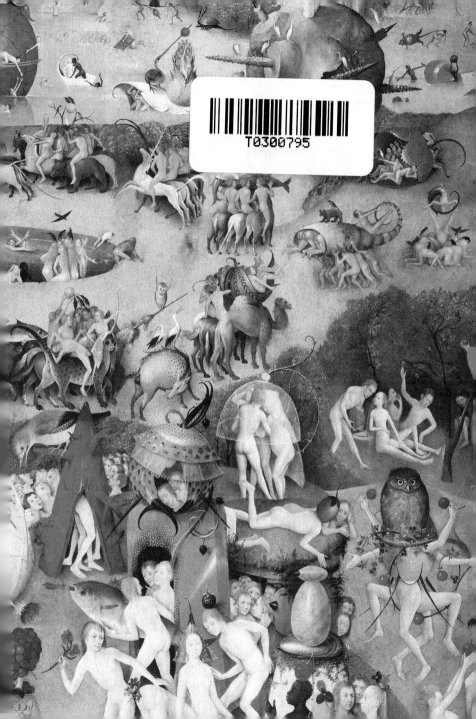

T0300795

WEIRD MEDIEVAL GUYS

5 7 9 10 8 6 4

Square Peg, an imprint of Vintage, is part of the Penguin Random House group of companies whose addresses can be found at global.penguinrandomhouse.com

First published by Square Peg in 2023

penguin.co.uk/vintage

Printed and bound by Livonia Print, Latvia

The authorised representative in the EEA is Penguin Random House Ireland, Morrison Chambers, 32 Nassau Street, Dublin D02 YH68

A CIP catalogue record for this book is available from the British Library

ISBN 9781529908305

WEIRD MEDIEVAL GUYS

OLIVIA M. SWARTHOUT

How to live, laugh, love (and die) in dark times

◼ SQUARE PEG

CONTENTS

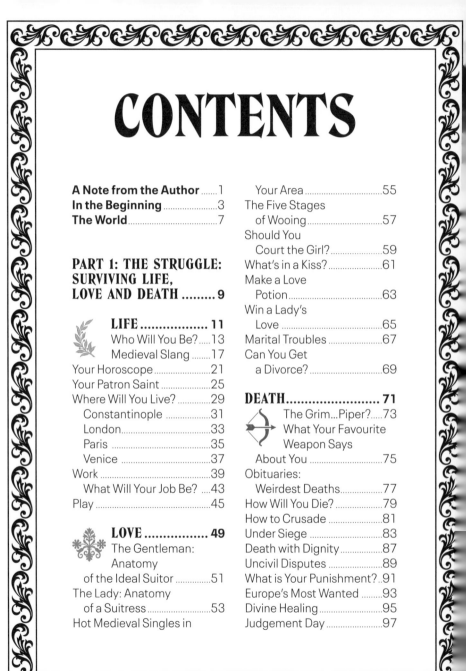

A NOTE FROM THE AUTHOR

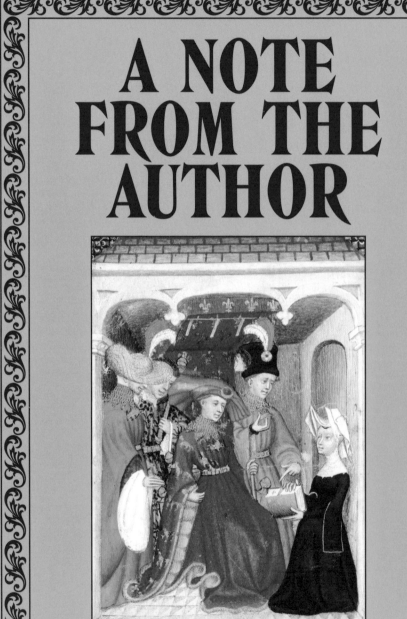

Most of the images and stories in this book come from manuscripts made between 500 and 1,500 years ago. All things considered, that's a very long time.

It's not easy to imagine what people were like a thousand years ago. Just think, then, how they'd feel looking a millennium into the future trying to imagine us. Our world would seem so strange to them. They didn't know about pizza delivery or the perils of online dating in your thirties. Most of them probably would never have guessed that we'd be able to access centuries of art and writing in an instant from a device called a 'phone' that weighs less than a turnip. If you could travel back to medieval Europe and tell someone that one day, in the distant future, their work could be seen by hundreds of thousands of people across the world, they probably would have said something like '*hwæt?*', which is Old English for '*what?*'

In April 2022, I began a Twitter account called 'weird medieval guys' in the hopes of shining a light on the oft-underappreciated world of medieval manuscripts and their art. Like a scribe of yore, I too scarcely expected to reach more than a handful of people with my work. To have over half a million of you following me now boggles the mind. At first, it was intimidating. I'm not a historian! I like history, but that doesn't make me a historian, unfortunately. But I did my best to share what I knew, and as I learned more, over half a million people got to learn with me.

For the most part, I am just a platform for the people who made these images. Illustrators of medieval manuscripts didn't create art with the expectation that it would be displayed in public. Books were rare, private items that few could read and fewer could afford. The art within them was made to inform, educate and entertain their reader while the book was open. Close it, and it was hidden away until the next time. Though smaller and simpler than the paintings of famous masters, manuscript art often feels more personal, like an unfiltered look into the medieval mind. A Rembrandt painting inspires awe, but a hastily sketched 13th-century drawing of a person punching a giant bat lets you share a laugh with a person from 700 years ago. For just a moment, that person feels real.

We can't talk to the artists any more, but I have tried to use WMG to give them a voice nonetheless. This book represents the culmination of those efforts. Though lacking in historical qualifications, I have as much as possible poured every ounce of love and respect for the medieval world into this book. The beliefs in it are not mine: I don't think that women are secretly snakes or that warriors in Egypt rode crocodiles down the Nile into battle. Nor do I present them uncritically: though we can laugh with medieval people, we can also laugh at them, and be grateful that our world has shed so many of the biases and falsehoods that went unchallenged for so long.

Enough from the 21st century, though. From the next page, listen not to me but to a weird medieval guy who wants you to understand their world.

IN THE

BEGINNING

In the beginning, there was nothing.
That much, most of us agree on. After that, it gets a bit trickier.
But for a long time, for a lot of people, this has been
how the story continues:

On the first day

He made darkness and light.

On the second day

He made the sky and the clouds.

On the third day

He made land, the sea and the plants.

On the fourth day

**He made the sun, the moon
and the stars.**

On the fifth day

**He made creatures of the sea,
creatures of the sky and insects.**

On the sixth day

**He made creatures of the earth, and,
most importantly, humans. God made humans
in His own image, and gave the rest of
creation to us ... A birthday gift, as it were.**

On the seventh day

He rested.

After that, we lived in a big garden together with all the animals and we even got to name them, because God somehow hadn't gotten around to that bit yet. There was no evil, no violence, no money, no anger and no shame. It was all pretty simple, but only for a little while. Unfortunately, we did the one thing we weren't supposed to do, and after that things were very different.

From then on, we had to figure everything out for ourselves, which has been a bit of a mixed bag. We had children, and they had children, and so on until the Earth was covered in people. We committed some crimes but we did some good things, too, and it mostly balanced out, hopefully.

God kept in touch, and He even came to visit us a couple of times.

The highs and lows of the first few thousand years

Although He didn't stay for very long.

We might have traded Paradise for an eternity of death and taxes, but it's not all that bad. God still made us in His image, and the rest of nature is still ours. In His infinite wisdom, perhaps foreseeing that the whole Eden setup was only going to last for so long, God left all sorts of warnings and lessons hidden in His creation for us to find. Everything in the world, from the way plants grow to the behaviour of beasts, is a reflection of the divine intelligence which made it. Although we are better than all other life on this Earth, that does not mean that we cannot watch and learn about everything below us in order to learn how to better ourselves, for just like humans, there is both great evil and great virtue in the creatures that walk, crawl, swim and fly. In the process, on the path to making sense of this planet, we may have written a book with information. It wasn't intended to inform, just to inspire. Let's hope it was received as such.

**Soon enough, God created everything.
Creating everything wasn't easy, though, so God
had to do it in bits**

THE WORLD

HERE IS A MAP OF THE KNOWN WORLD
IN AD 1490, AS SEEN FROM FLORENCE

PART 1

THE STRUGGLE: SURVIVING LIFE, LOVE AND DEATH

LIFE
Creatures That
Walk the Earth

LOVE
Creatures That
Fly the Heavens

DEATH
Creatures That
Swim the Seas

LIFE

Remember how, in the beginning, you were given the whole Earth, AND all of nature, AND every living thing? Now the world is yours for the taking, and it's time to see what it has to offer! It's time to start your own weird medieval life. Most people only get one shot at life, so cherish this opportunity to start afresh and carve out a place for yourself in the world.

Welcome to LIFE!

WHO WILL YOU BE?

If you want to start a life in the Middle Ages, you'll need a proper name, not a daft modern one. Sure, lots of medieval Europeans were called things like John and Maria and Catherine, but don't you want something with a bit more *pizazz*? Of course you do.

Let's start with a first name. Go to the row numbered with the day of your birth to find out what you'll be called from now on. Choose the name that suits you best from any of the three columns and say hello to your new medieval self![1]

---

1. Gender-neutral names were extremely uncommon in the Middle Ages as most names had dedicated masculine and feminine versions. As such, the third column is made of medieval nouns and adjectives that nevertheless make for very good names.

	Male names	Female names	Names for everyone
1	Bertwin	Swanhilde	Dorian
2	Valerian	Illuminata	Columba
3	Winegod	Yolanda	Wuldor
4	Zenobius	Peregrina	Sinister
5	Boguslav	Sibyl	Sweven
6	Odelhard	Hildegard	Azorp
7	Prospero	Abba	Galiard
8	Quieton	Admiranda	Belphegor
9	Ratbald	Aurofina	Gingivere
10	Seaborn	Griselda	Nedder
11	Tanquard	Clotilda	Newte
12	Thorkill	Lettice	Squamous
13	Gangwolf	Gundred	Strangelyn
14	Gumbert	Millicent	Azedam
15	Guy	Beatrix	Azolemode
16	Humiliosus	Wulfeva	Wernard
17	Dragomir	Wulfwynn	Darklyng
18	Odo	Wigfled	Daungerous
19	Crispin	Bonissima	Frankeleyn
20	Bonjohn	Euphrosyne	Gunge
21	Evergrim	Herberta	Hoskin
22	Halfdan	Frigg	Rubin
23	Helmhard	Morbida	Galerous
24	Oswain	Petronilla	Zelen
25	Laslob	Amabel	Wangtooth
26	Gotboldus	Grimberg	Ernestful
27	Thaddeus	Jeronima	Boffet
28	Balthazar	Primavera	Radwise
29	Mold	Apollonia	Valentine
30	Meingod	Agnes	Avis
31	Manwulf	Borbala	Josian

Adjectives	Nouns
Merke: Dark	**Dastard**: Wretch, vile fellow
Od: Odd	**Chere**: Face, expression, appearance
Gryndel: Wrathful	**Botme**: Bottom
Moyst: Moist	**Fet**: Feet
Knokled: Knobbed, rugged	**Wytt**: Mind, intelligence
Madde: Mad, insane	**Chorl**: Common man
Addle: Rotten	**Wyf**: Wife
Prest: Prompt, quick	**Housebonde**: Husband
Abhomynable: Abominable	**Shone**: Shoes
Wys: Wise	**Nese**: Nose
Myghty: Mighty	**Gost**: Soul, spirit
Onest: Trustworthy	**Schrewe**: A wicked old woman
Greate: Great, large	**Boonyes**: Bones
Biwyled: Deluded	**Wreche**: Vengeance
Trewe: Honest, faithful	**Lemman**: Lover
Ferly: Wonderful	**Huerte**: Heart
Huly: Slow	**Carpyng**: Talking
Abd: Worshipper of	

Now, you probably have a surname, but those haven't been around for ever! In the Middle Ages, a lot of people didn't have a family name, but at a time when up to 35 per cent of men were named John, this could get confusing. This is where your *byname* comes in! A byname is a nickname that usually says something about your appearance, behaviour or origin. You usually didn't get to choose it, though – like most nicknames, your peers would decide on the name that most aptly suited you and you were stuck with it.

In the medieval tradition, please ask a friend or trusted colleague to choose an adjective and noun from the list on the left that they think describes you best.

Put them together into one word and that's your byname. Next up, stick your first name and your byname together and you're on your way to becoming a local!

MEDIEVAL SLANG: AN A–Z OF MIDDLE ENGLISH

A name is a good start, but you're going to need to learn a bit of local lingo as well. Here are a few medieval words that will have you sounding like a native in no time.

**AGAINWEND
(ENGLISH, VERB)**
To retreat

**BESMUT
(ENGLISH, VERB)**
To defile

**CUCURBITARIUS
(LATIN, NOUN)**
A lover of gourds and squash

**DEARWORTH
(ENGLISH, ADJ.)**
Precious or very valuable

**EARMING
(ENGLISH, NOUN)**
A wretched being

Two guys being gadelings, England, 14th century

FULGETRUM
(LATIN, NOUN)
A flash of lightning

GADELING
(ENGLISH, NOUN)
A comrade, fellow or vagabond

GILEYSPEKE
(ENGLISH, NOUN)
A cunning trick or illusion

GLOMBEN
(ENGLISH, VERB)
To look downcast or glum; to frown

GRAVILOQUUS
(LATIN, NOUN)
A man who speaks gravely
and seriously

HALOPHANTA
(LATIN, NOUN)
A talented liar

INANIMUS
(LATIN, ADJ.)
Without soul; lifeless

JUGULARE
MORTUOS
(LATIN, VERB)
To kick someone while they're down;
literally 'to cut the throat of corpses'

LINGULACA
(LATIN, NOUN)
A woman who speaks
excessively

LIVERSOON
(ENGLISH, NOUN)
Food or sustenance

MAGNALIA
(LATIN, NOUN)
Great things to be
wondered at

MALEFICUS
(LATIN, NOUN)
One who does harm
to others

MEROBIBA
(LATIN, NOUN)
A woman who enjoys
very strong wine

**A merobiba's average
Friday night**

METHFUL
(ENGLISH, ADJ.)
Peaceful, quiet
or modest

NOUMBLES
(ENGLISH, NOUN)
The entrails of a beast,
especially a deer

OBIURGATRIX
(LATIN, NOUN)
A woman who loves
to chide or rebuke

ORGULOUS
(ENGLISH, ADJ.)
Proud or haughty
to excess

OVERWERP
(ENGLISH, VERB)
To boil over,
as a pot

PEEKGOOSE
(ENGLISH, NOUN)
Someone who
is silly or a simpleton

PHILOLOGUS
(LATIN, NOUN)
A lover of words

PROSERPERE
(LATIN, VERB)
To creep about
like a serpent

SCORTOR
(LATIN, VERB)
To spend time in the
company of harlots

STERILIS AMATOR
(LATIN, NOUN)
A lover who has no money

WREKER
(ENGLISH, NOUN)
One who avenges

WRAKEFUL
(ENGLISH, ADJ.)
Wicked

A philologus in his natural habitat

'I hope you find my music to be most ... methful'

YOUR HOROSCOPE

Astrology was very important in the Middle Ages and could be used to tell you all about the weather, crops, and other natural phenomena. The position that the stars were in at the time of your birth has long been said to influence who you are as a person, too.

Let's see what the medieval stars say about you!

♈ ARIES ♂
(March 21–April 19)

Element: Fire
Planet: Mars

You are courageous and unafraid to speak your mind in even the most dire of situations, which makes you a massive liability to yourself and others. The number of tavern fights you've been in is large and the number you've lost is only slightly smaller.

♉ TAURUS ♀
(April 20–May 20)

Element: Earth
Planet: Venus

You are a capable, intelligent person and use the majority of your time and energy coming up with ways to avoid your responsibilities. Everyone thinks you're a complete simpleton and expects very little of you. That's exactly what you want them to think.

♊ GEMINI ☿
(May 21–June 21)

Element: Air
Planet: Mercury

You are a very likeable type who has many friends and few enemies – that you know of. Your friends assure you that no one is secretly out to get you, which is exactly what they *would* say if they *were* secretly out to get you, isn't it?

♋ CANCER ☾
(June 22–July 22)

Element: Water
Planet: The Moon

Your true nature is a bit of a mystery to all but your closest friends, who know you as a deeply intuitive and insightful person – almost supernaturally so. Not that you have dark supernatural powers, of course. Right?

♌ LEO ☉
(July 23–August 22)

Element: Fire
Planet: the Sun
You are rather vain and love to be the star of the show, which has gotten you kicked out of more than one juggling troupe. You need a steady stream of love and attention at all times and will wither away like a parched flower without it.

♍ VIRGO ☿
(August 23–September 22)

Element: Earth
Planet: Mercury
You are seen as rather frigid and distant by some, but deep down you are slightly less frigid and distant than they think.
You actually have a lot of friends, but most of them are trees, stars, animals and books.

♎ LIBRA ♀
(September 23–October 23)

Element: Air
Planet: Venus
You are a very kind and generous soul, who sees the best in everyone they meet. You are always courting at least five different suitors, but you make sure that they never find out about each other. As a kind and caring person, you'd hate to make them upset.

♏ SCORPIO ♂
(October 24–November 21)

Element: Water
Planet: Mars
You are intimidating to your enemies and even more intimidating to your friends, who go to great lengths to keep you happy. Sadly, you don't realise this and think that it's just your natural charm at work. It's not.

♐ SAGITTARIUS ♄
(November 22–December 21)

Element: Fire
Planet: Jupiter
You care deeply about truth
and knowledge and can never
say no to a good debate.
Unfortunately, you struggle
to find debating partners
as wise and enlightened
as yourself.

♑ CAPRICORN ♃
(December 22–January 19)

Element: Earth
Planet: Saturn
You are a deeply moral person
who works very hard, and the
world would be a better place if
everyone was like you. People
know this but won't admit it
because they find your smug-
ness unbearable.

♒ AQUARIUS ♄
(January 20–February 18)

Element: Air
Planet: Saturn
You are a senseless optimist who truly
believes there is good in the world
despite overwhelming evidence to the
contrary. You're too clever for your own
good and will probably one day become
either a king or a clown. If anyone could
be both at once, it's you.

♓ PISCES ♃
(February 19–March 20)

Element: Water
Planet: Jupiter
You have the soul of an artist and
would do well to pursue music,
painting or poetry because of
your sensitive, thoughtful nature.
In other words, you wouldn't
make it through a single day of
hard labour in the turnip fields.

YOUR
PATRON SAINT

The stars aren't the only guidance
you'll need throughout your weird medieval life.
It's a good idea to have a patron saint, a heavenly
protector who you can call upon in times of great need.
Different saints specialise in helping people out
with different things. Have a look through
and see if you can find one that appeals to you.

1. AMANDUS

Patron saint of wine makers, beer brewers and innkeepers

Those patrons who get way too drunk and won't leave at closing time? Sounds like a problem for Amandus!

2. ALBINUS

Patron saint for protection against pirate attacks

'No need to thank me, guys, not seeing you beautiful people get murdered by pirates is its own reward.'

3. DROGO

Patron saint of ugly people and shepherds

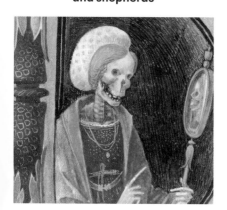

Just remember that beauty is only skin deep.

4. ZITA

Patron saint of lost keys

'Wow, it was in my pocket this whole time.'

5. ANTHONY OF PADUA

Patron saint of all lost objects, lost people, lost souls and those who hope to find love

Don't pray too hard to Anthony or you might start finding things you hadn't lost in the first place, like dragons.

6. SWITHUN

Patron saint of the weather

'Well, *someone* must be praying for it.'

7. GUINEFORT

Patron saint of small children and the only dog to have ever been worshipped as a saint

And he was a very good boy, too.

8. GENESIUS

Patron saint of clowns and comedians

'This time I'm not joking, I really do have a patron saint!'

9. DENIS

Patron saint for protection against hydrophobia

'Hey, Denis, are you sure this is the best way to get over my fear of water?'

10. QUENTIN

Patron saint for protection against coughs and sneezes

Frog in your throat?
There's a saint for that.

11. BARBARA

Patron saint of fire, lightning and explosions

Fire is great for justice and vengeance, but it's even better for baking bread.

12. BASIL

Patron saint of exorcisms

Of course, if Basil doesn't answer your prayers, you can always try banishing the demon by hitting it with a big stick.

WHERE WILL YOU LIVE?

You've got the basics worked out, for the most part, so it's time to launch your medieval life. But where shall you start from? Answer this simple quiz and you'll soon find out which medieval city your heart belongs to. Your adventure begins here!

If you could have any animal's ability, what would it be?

A. The owl's ability to turn its head around backwards
B. The pig's ability to eat acorns raw
C. The snail's ability to make its own slime
D. The frog's ability to hibernate in ponds all winter

Do you have faith in the power of friendship?

A. Most of my friends are also my enemies
B. I could not have survived my many struggles without friendship
C. That's stupid
D. Friendship forever!

What do you look for in a romantic partner?

A. Someone who will protect me and make me feel safe
B. Someone who loves me despite my many quirks
C. Someone well read and educated
D. Someone cultured and refined who loves to socialise

What sin do you commit the most often?

A. I get road rage when people ride their donkeys too slowly
B. I say the Lord's name in vain every goddamn day
C. I secretly think Geoff's wife is a total babe
D. I can never say no to another pheasant pie

How frequently do you pray?

A. I'm praying right now
B. I've prayed at least once before in my life
C. I pray at church every week
D. I only pray when I want something

Now, tally up how many of each letter you got! If you got mostly ...

A: You're made to live in Constantinople! Go to page 31 to learn more about your new home.

B: It's time to pack your bags and move to London! Go to page 33 to learn more about your new home.

C: You're a born Parisian! Go to page 35 to learn more about your new home.

D: You would fit in perfectly in Venice! Go to page 37 to learn more about your new home.

ANATOMY OF CONSTANTINOPLE

COUNTRY: Byzantine Empire
YEAR: 1450 **POPULATION:** approx. 50,000

THE BYZANTINE TIMES

Rioters burn down city
after chariot race takes a turn

8 MARCH 562

Byzantines love their horse races and have passionate factions based on their favourite chariot teams, but this time our love of the sport went too far. After a close call at the races, war broke out between chariot factions and over the next few days, the rioters killed thousands, burned down much of the city, and laid siege to the Royal Palace. Now that the emperor's soldiers have restored the peace, the final death toll stands at around 30,000. Our hearts go out to all those who have lost loved ones to this terrible tragedy.

1. Constantinople's famous walls, which only succumbed to a few Crusades over the centuries. You'll feel nice and safe here!

2. The Hippodrome, famous chariot racing arena and primary source of entertainment.

3. The Hagia Sophia, the biggest mosque in the World, not the worst place in the World to pray!

4. The Royal Palace, occupying a desirable space right next to the Hippodrome.

5. The Maiden's Tower, so called because a legend tells of a noble maiden who died there.

6. Pera, the European side of Constantinople.

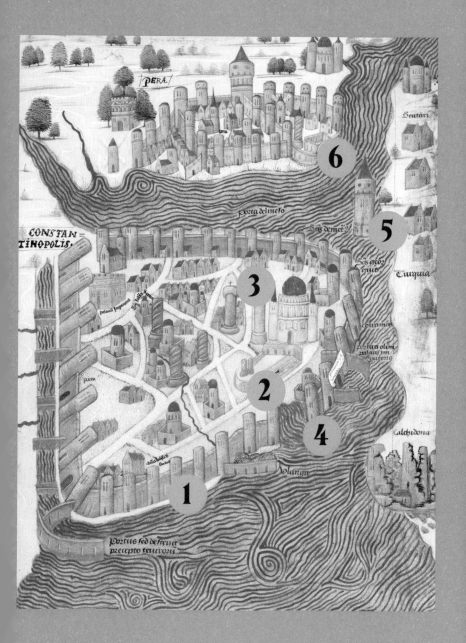

PERA.

CONSTAN=
TINOPOLIS.

Porta del meto

Scutari

Turquia

Calchidona

Portus sed destruct
precepto teutronis

ANATOMY OF LONDON

COUNTRY: England **YEAR:** 1415 **POPULATION:** approx. 50,000

THE DAILY LONDINIUM
3 FEBRUARY 1101

Bishop Ranulf Flambard was the first ever prisoner to be held in the Tower of London. Today, six months after his imprisonment, Ranulf became the first ever person to escape from the Tower of London and is now on the lam. Guards are currently searching for his whereabouts. Report any sightings to your local Sheriff.

OBITUARY: ROGER STYWARD
8 AUGUST 1326

An eel merchant named Roger Styward threw a bucket full of eel skins onto the street beside two merchants' shops. The apprentices of the shopkeepers promptly emerged and assaulted Roger, who died shortly thereafter of his injuries.

1. The River Thames, London's main waterway and primary dumping place for sewage and rubbish.

2. The old London Bridge. Houses were built on it so their rents could be used to pay for the bridge's upkeep.

3. The Tower of London, a fortress, prison, castle and symbol of monarchic self-importance since the 1100s. If you commit any acts of treason, which is basically doing anything the monarch doesn't like, you can expect to see the inside very quickly.

4. The Traitors' Gate, an entrance to the Tower accessible only by boat. (Occasionally used by non-traitors, too.)

5. Most Londoners live in small apartments within larger houses built of wood and straw, which are rather prone to bursting into flames at the slightest spark.

33

ANATOMY OF PARIS

COUNTRY: France **YEAR:** 1450 **POPULATION:** approx. 150,000

THE ORIFLAMME THE ICE AND WOLVES RETURN

18 DECEMBER 1338

The River Seine has frozen over again, and wolves from beyond Paris have re-entered the city over the ice to dig up corpses and attack poor Parisians. Remember: if you see a wolf before it sees you, immediately strip naked. See page 107 of the Bestiary for more advice on keeping safe from wolves.

1. The River Seine, Paris' largest waterway. It serves as both the primary source of drinking water and the primary receptacle of sewerage for the city. How convenient!

2. Pont St Michel, which like London Bridge doubled as a real estate opportunity.

3. The Notre-Dame. Ah, what could be more Parisian? Close to 300 years old at this point, but she doesn't look a day over 150.

4. Demons, also known as Parisians.

ANATOMY OF VENICE

COUNTRY: The Republic of Venice
YEAR: 1500 **POPULATION:** approx. 100,000

THE DAILY GONDOLIER

New rules for choosing new ruler

24 APRIL 1268

Concerns over corruption in elections of the Doge have led the Great Council of Venice to enact a new procedure for selecting our glorious ruler. Rather than letting the Council choose the electors, the new process will go as follows:

Thirty members of the Great Council, chosen by lot, will be reduced by lot to nine.

The nine choose forty and the forty are reduced by lot to twelve, who choose twenty-five.

The twenty-five are reduced by lot to nine, and the nine elect forty-five.

These forty-five are once more reduced by lot to eleven.

The eleven finally choose the forty-one who elect the Doge.

1. The Piazza San Marco, a grand square decorated with marble and pillars stolen from Constantinople. Aren't you glad you don't live there?

2. Are you afraid of water? I hope not! There are over 150 canals in Venice. Don't worry, though, they only rise to flood the city once or twice every year.

3. 'Venetian' means quality, so ships come to Venice to export fine fabrics, art and other luxuries around the world.

4. Venice doesn't have a king, queen or emperor. Instead, you'll swear fealty to the Doge, who's chosen democratically by the aristocrats to rule for life.

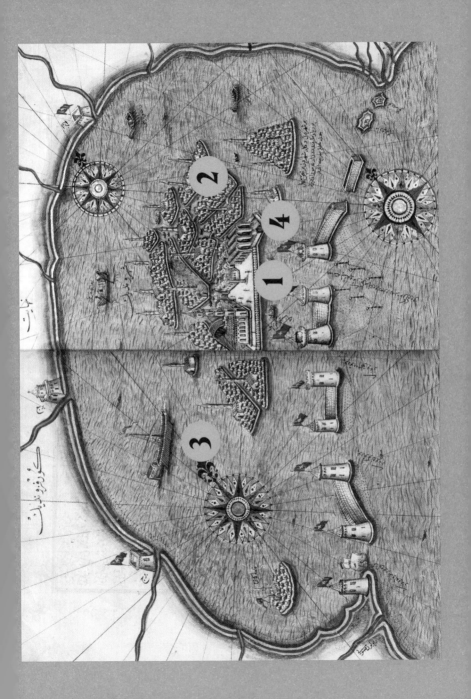

WORK

Everyone has to do it! People in the Middle Ages usually did the same thing for their whole life, and would teach their trade to their children, who would also do the same thing their whole lives. Bad news for you if your parents were leech collectors or sewage cleaners, but then again, those jobs are important!

Join the clergy if you love hats

An army or several is a must for
defending the kingdom and keeping
all those pesky commoners in line

Blacksmiths are important
for making things like tools,
horseshoes and babies

There's a place for creative
types, too! You can always
become a professional fool

Not much of a
people person?
Become a scholar!

Art, of course, is a noble pursuit

Monk is a good option if you think you'd look good with a tonsure

Someone needs to keep the animals in line, too – that hen looks ready to fight

WHAT WILL YOUR JOB BE?

Assuming you survive past infancy, you're going to need to start working soon. What will you spend the rest of your days doing? Here's a helpful quiz to find out:

Oh no! Your village is being burnt down by Viking raiders! You have to escape now and don't have much time to pack. What item do you make sure to bring?
A. A book of epic poetry so I can keep myself occupied
B. Some cheese and rye bread so I don't go hungry
C. My best friend so I don't get lonely
D. Nothing, I let it all burn down to the ground

The people in your life who you appreciate most are:
A. People who have similar interests to mine and love to have deep conversations
B. My pets
C. People who work hard and inspire me to do my best
D. People who respect my space and privacy

Which of your good qualities tends to impress your peers and make your enemies seethe with envy?

A. I am bound by my honour code and would never renege on my vow of fealty to my lord

B. I do not judge those around me, least of all sinners and harlots

C. I possess razor-sharp intuition and am always able to keep one step ahead of my foes

D. I am a constant dispenser of wise counsel and can always be trusted to provide valuable advice to those in distress

You've just left the baker's. When you look in your bag you notice that he gave you one roll less than you asked for, even though you paid the full price. How do you respond?

A. I go back to the shop to let him know

B. I immediately eat one of the rolls and give the baker a hard time for giving me *two* rolls less than I asked for – that'll show him!

C. I don't say anything, but I start going to a different bakery from that day on

D. The baker probably is struggling to make ends meet for his family, so it's not his fault if he's trying to increase his profit margins. I go back to the shop and give my bread back, telling him that he can keep my money, too

On feast days when you are mandated not to work, how do you choose to spend your time?

A. Watching the mummers and jesters perform

B. Partaking in a festive cake or several

C. Consuming more ale than anyone else in the tavern

D. Enjoying the peace and quiet

Now tally
up those
answers!
If you got
mostly ...

A: You're a born scribe!

B: Your destiny is to become a swineherd!

C: You'd be a perfect innkeeper!

D: Your best bet is to become a hermit! You don't tend to indulge in worldly comfort because you spend your time deep in thought or helping other people.

PLAY

Before you get too worried, there's lots of time for fun, too. You can look forward to having every Sunday off, plus another 40 or so days of Church holidays. Easter and Christmas, of course, as well as Candlemas, Pentecost, Ascension Day, Epiphany, All Saints' Day, Assumption of Mary, Corpus Christi, Feast of the Sacred Heart, and more! Of course, you won't be able to work once the sun has gone down (have you ever tried to plough a field by candle light?), so no one will blame you for clocking off and grabbing a tankard of ale with your pals whenever it gets dark.

Gambling isn't strictly allowed, but are you going to let that stop you?

If you've got blue blood, you can have a tilt at jousting

If you're looking for something more relaxing to do, just pour yourself a drink

Everyone loves a bit of music,
even the dog

But not horn music,
dogs hate horn music

Worms are known to
enjoy a bit of fiddle

Be careful about playing
chess with monkeys:
they're notorious cheats

**If all else fails, have a nap – on your own,
or with friends**

Impress your friends with some sweet dance moves

LOVE

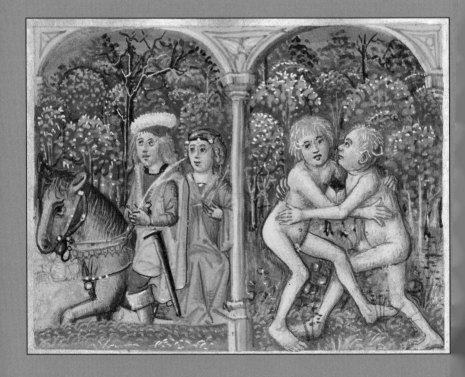

OK, so you're still alive. Well done. But don't you think your newfangled life would be even better with a *special friend?* Sure, love brings its own difficulties, but nevertheless we humans keep shamelessly coming back to it. It's hard to say exactly why, but there must be something about it that we need in our lives – that, or we just love to self-inflict pain.[1]

Remember this as you flick through the next few pages, because it may be your only chance at avoiding a crushed soul and lonely death – the likelihood of you dying, and dying young at that (more on this later) – is incredibly high. But to make living all the more worthwhile, go and enjoy LOVE!

---

1. Or perhaps it's the pheromones. But what do I know? I'm not God. And science is still in its burgeoning form.

THE GENTLEMAN: ANATOMY OF THE IDEAL SUITOR

It's a burden to be a man in this world.
Even if you manage to find a virtuous woman
among all the sinning temptresses out there,
it's still your job to charm her with your
handsome looks and gallant ways.

Here's what you need
to become irresistible
to your lady love.

1.

Golden blond is the ideal hair colour, and it's even better if you cut it into a chic bowl haircut, or a pudding-basin cut, as it's often called.

2.

You don't need to be as pale as a lady, but do try not to get too much sun. The Sun is the closest thing to Hell you can experience while on our flat and dinky Earth!

3.

You get a houppelande, too, (see page 54), but go for knee length. A bright red fabric is sure to make you look vital, regal and powerful, and a contrasting fur lining will make all the court ladies go, 'Wow, did he kill all those weasels himself?'

4.

Keep a dagger on you at all times. You never know when you might need to stab a rival. Or a weasel.

5.

Hunting, riding and training should keep your calves nice and shapely, but don't let them get too big. Try to give off the vibe that you take care of your body, but still leave plenty of time for prayer and quiet contemplation.

6.

No outfit is complete without the perfect pair of hose: tight woollen stockings that will put your calves on full display. Two-coloured hose will call extra attention to those perfectly formed legs. If anyone says you look like a court jester, stab them.

THE LADY: ANATOMY OF A SUITRESS

Whether rich or poor,
a lady should always put her
beauty first. After all, how
else is she to prove her value
to a man? A few key traits
define the ideal woman.

1.
The hennin, a tall headdress made of fabric wrapped around wire, is an absolute necessity.

2.
Nothing is more feminine than a big forehead! (Beauty hack: if you're not naturally endowed, you can pluck or shave the hair on your forehead back a few centimetres.)

3.
In fact, the less hair on your face, the better. (Pro tip: pluck your eyebrows thin or get rid of them entirely for a more youthful face.)

4.
To emphasise your innocent appearance, you should have a slender nose, pointy chin, small mouth and ears, and big eyes. Try to look fragile. Like a sexy egg. (Men like eggs, right ...?)

5.
Keep out of the sun to maintain pale, smooth, flawless skin. Blemishes, moles, freckles and other impurities of the skin signify an impurity of the soul. Or possibly smallpox. In either case, not good.

6.
Signify your high social status with an expensive blue houppelande, a long, loose gown with wide, flowing sleeves.

7.
Also, being Caucasian helps.

HOT MEDIEVAL SINGLES IN YOUR AREA

Handsome monk last week – grow out that tonsure for me?

When I saw you walking into the abbey for morning prayer in those dashing brown robes, I couldn't help but think that it must be lonely spending all those long nights in the company of other men. I know you promised yourself to the service of the Lord. But maybe we could promise ourselves to each other instead?

– ABBY WITHOUT AN E

Looking for a charmer, not a farmer

Widow, 36, seeking well-off gent who can provide a comfortable living for me and my six cats. Sick of all these peasant boys wasting my time. I need a real gentleman who owns land and knows what to do with it. Must be literate (my favourite book is *Beowulf*). Must like cats.

A beautiful lady needs an able swordsman

To the striking young lady whose knight was unhorsed in the first round of the joust. We made brief eye contact and you shook your head as if to say 'can you believe this guy?' I felt his performance was shameful, too, and thought you might be interested in a lancer with a bit more skill. I won't fall from my horse, but I'd love to fall for you.

– YOUR LANCELOT

Unhinged: Retired Crusader looking for next conquest

Middle-aged bachelor (21), well travelled, passionate about the Lord. Just got back from the Holy Land to discover my front door was unhinged. Turns out my wife had moved in with the blacksmith next door. It was a hammer blow but I'm looking to move on with a pious, devoted lady who will accompany me on my next military campaign so I can keep an eye on her. Cheating harlots need not enquire.

THE FIVE STAGES OF WOOING

You might be looking for love,
but have you even thought about what
type of love you're after? Didn't think so.
Not all love is created equal, you see.

As the well-to-do member of society that one can only presume you are, you have a couple of options: marriage and courtship.

1.

IDENTIFICATION

Use your wisdom and discernment
to identify the perfect romantic
prospect, or the most eligible among
the 50 people in your village.
Parental or landlord approval
may be required.

2.

PURSUIT

Put your natural charm and good graces to work, or just follow the advice in the next pages.

3.

CONTACT

Finally, all your courting paid off, and you can finally be together! Now is the time for swooning, fawning and a magical first kiss. Just try to keep it chaste, because if things go too far, it's time for a ...

4.

MARRIAGE

It's time to make things official! Exchange rings and vows, drink and dance, and then finally it's time for that consummation you've been waiting for. You did wait till marriage, right?

5.

EVERYTHING ELSE

After that, it's up to you how things go. Love each other, hate each other, have babies, have affairs, accuse each other of witchcraft – there are plenty of great options!

SHOULD YOU COURT THE GIRL?

Can't decide whether to go ahead with the relationship? Here's a handy guide!

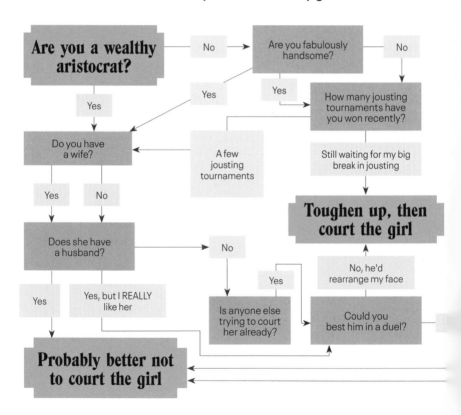

Are you a wealthy aristocrat?

No → Are you fabulously handsome?

No →

Yes → Do you have a wife?

Yes → Are you fabulously handsome?

Yes → How many jousting tournaments have you won recently?

A few jousting tournaments

Still waiting for my big break in jousting

Do you have a wife?

Yes → Does she have a husband?

No →

Toughen up, then court the girl

Does she have a husband?

No → Is anyone else trying to court her already?

Yes → Yes, but I REALLY like her

Yes →

No, he'd rearrange my face

Yes →

Is anyone else trying to court her already?

Could you best him in a duel?

Probably better not to court the girl

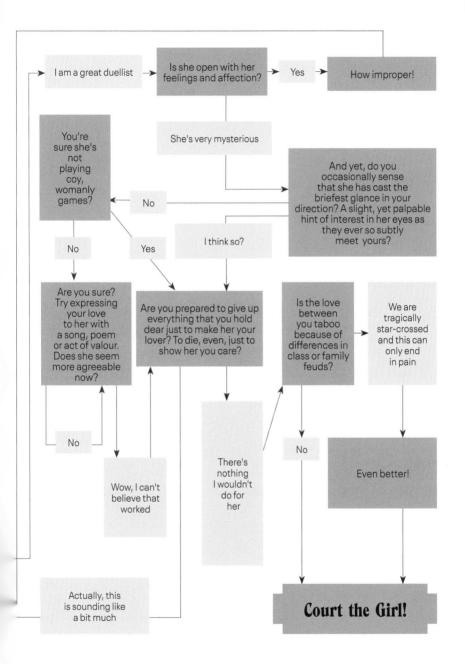

I am a great duellist → Is she open with her feelings and affection? → Yes → How improper!

She's very mysterious

And yet, do you occasionally sense that she has cast the briefest glance in your direction? A slight, yet palpable hint of interest in her eyes as they ever so subtly meet yours?

You're sure she's not playing coy, womanly games?

No

I think so?

No

Yes

Are you sure? Try expressing your love to her with a song, poem or act of valour. Does she seem more agreeable now?

Are you prepared to give up everything that you hold dear just to make her your lover? To die, even, just to show her you care?

Is the love between you taboo because of differences in class or family feuds?

We are tragically star-crossed and this can only end in pain

No

Wow, I can't believe that worked

There's nothing I wouldn't do for her

No

Even better!

Actually, this is sounding like a bit much

Court the Girl!

WHAT'S IN A KISS?

Kissing in the Middle Ages wasn't reserved for husbands and wives, and a kiss could carry all kinds of meanings. Greeting someone, showing respect, sealing a deal – all great times to sneak a quick peck in. Here's a guide to a few types of kisses, should you encounter them on your journey.

Kissing a lady while she's at work doing manual labour – or any kind of labour – is generally regarded as bad etiquette

If an angel kisses you,
you must have done something
to impress them. They don't just
kiss anyone, angels

Kissing your enemy
after declaring a truce:
royal wedding on
the horizon?

Kiss someone while betraying
them so the whole world knows
you're a scoundrel

You can kiss your superior's foot to
remind them that you're their loyal
footman

MAKE A
LOVE POTION

If things aren't working out with your sweetheart, it might be time to turn to alternative methods. All you need is this one simple aphrodisiac ingredient and she'll be head over heels before you know it. Only one small issue – the secret ingredient is a mandrake root, which can potentially be deadly to harvest.

Follow these instructions closely and you will hopefully make it out with your life and your romance intact.

INGREDIENTS

* One dog
* One rope
* One hunting horn
* One ivory stake
* One mandrake root
growing in the ground

TIME

Three minutes

YIELD

One mandrake root

METHOD

1. Stay FAR AWAY from the mandrake root at all times when possible. It resembles a small, green man made of roots but when it is pulled out from its slumber, the mandrake emits a piercing wail so loud and shrill that all who hear go mad or die. Or possibly they go mad and then die.

2. Use the ivory stake to carefully dig around the top of the mandrake plant without exposing too much of the root.

3. Tie one end of the rope to your dog and the other to the mandrake.

4. Now, grab your hunting horn and run away as quickly as you can. While you're running, blow on the horn as loud as you possibly can. This will drown out the unearthly screeching of the little root man, provided you have decent lungs. The horn will also frighten the dog into running away, allowing the two of you to escape safely with your now-harmless mandrake root.

5. The mandrake root can be used in any aphrodisiac recipe of your choosing.

WIN A
LADY'S LOVE

1.

Impale a few men
in front of her to catch her
attention at the tourney.

2.

She's probably still not convinced of
your valour, so impale something bigger
and more dangerous, like a sea monster.

3.

Succeed in getting her to agree to a date, only to find out that she's not allowed out of the house without a chaperone. After a few more impalements, you may earn polite applause.

4.

Take a good, long look at yourself in the mirror and ask if this is all really worth it. Don't you have something better to be doing? Of course you don't!

5.

Finally manage to take her to a more secluded spot. Or so you think. Try to ignore her relatives in the bushes while you compare her beauty to the delicate roses.

6.

Congratulate her on her child-bearing proportions while she's trying to play her harp-lute.

MARITAL TROUBLES

Once the knot is tied, the rest of the struggle has just begun. There's no promise you'll always be happy with the person you married. Once the seeds of discontent are sown, it only goes downhill.

Here are a few signs of a(n) (f)ailing relationship.

If he buys the wrong ring size, it's a bad start to the marriage

If she gives you a secret haircut while you're asleep to take away your powers, it may be time to speak with a couples' counsellor

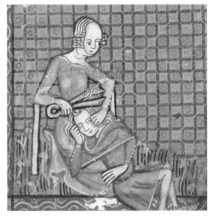

If she plants giant poison ivy to keep you out, you should probably have a talk

CAN YOU GET
A DIVORCE?

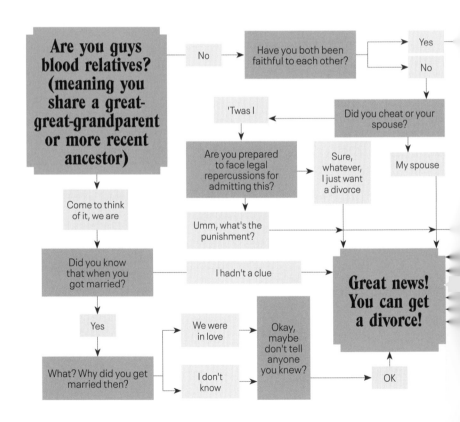

Are you guys blood relatives? (meaning you share a great-great-grandparent or more recent ancestor)

No → Have you both been faithful to each other?

→ Yes

→ No

Did you cheat or your spouse?

'Twas I

My spouse

Are you prepared to face legal repercussions for admitting this?

Sure, whatever, I just want a divorce

Umm, what's the punishment?

Come to think of it, we are

Did you know that when you got married?

I hadn't a clue

Yes

Great news! You can get a divorce!

What? Why did you get married then?

We were in love

I don't know

Okay, maybe don't tell anyone you knew?

OK

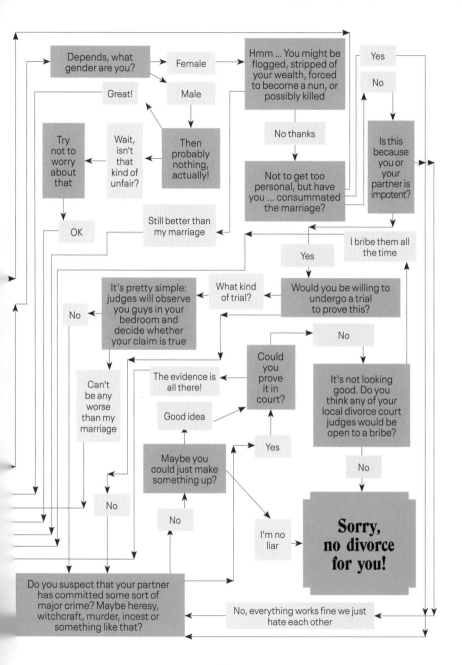

Depends, what gender are you? → Female → Hmm ... You might be flogged, stripped of your wealth, forced to become a nun, or possibly killed

Female → Male

Male → Then probably nothing, actually!

Then probably nothing, actually! → Wait, isn't that kind of unfair?

Wait, isn't that kind of unfair? → Great!

Wait, isn't that kind of unfair? → Try not to worry about that → OK

Hmm ... You might be flogged... → No thanks

Yes

No

No thanks → Not to get too personal, but have you ... consummated the marriage?

Is this because you or your partner is impotent?

Still better than my marriage

I bribe them all the time

Yes → Would you be willing to undergo a trial to prove this?

Would you be willing to undergo a trial to prove this? → What kind of trial?

What kind of trial? → It's pretty simple: judges will observe you guys in your bedroom and decide whether your claim is true

No

It's pretty simple... → Can't be any worse than my marriage

Can't be any worse than my marriage → No

No → It's not looking good. Do you think any of your local divorce court judges would be open to a bribe?

Could you prove it in court?

The evidence is all there!

Good idea

Could you prove it in court? → Yes

It's not looking good... → No

Maybe you could just make something up?

No

I'm no liar

Sorry, no divorce for you!

Do you suspect that your partner has committed some sort of major crime? Maybe heresy, witchcraft, murder, incest or something like that?

No, everything works fine we just hate each other

DEATH

I hope you enjoyed LOVE, but it's time to move on to something a bit more permanent. You might have guessed that it was going to end this way, but don't worry, you're still allowed to be sad. This isn't the end of your story, though. What comes next is hard to say unless you've been there before, but we'll probably all see each other on the other side.

Hope you've had fun and are ready for DEATH.

THE GRIM ...
PIPER?

For most of human history, people have tended to agree that the prospect of dying isn't particularly appealing. And yet, it's something we'll all have to do at least once. So why not try to make dying a bit more of a laugh? In the Late Middle Ages, a new genre of art began to develop: the *Danse Macabre*, or Dance of Death. *Danse Macabre* artwork depicts a skeletal personification of death leading people of all ages and walks of life in a dance to their graves – occasionally with musical accompaniment.

'Bagpipes? No thank you. Send a skeleton who knows how to play something nicer, please'

'We're going to have lots of fun together'

'I want to see you balance *two* cups on your head before I agree to follow you into the abyss'

'If you think I'm just going to waltz on into the afterlife with you ... you're absolutely correct!'

'Do you think you could come to terms with your impending demise on the way there? My snail is getting hungry'

'Trust me: I'm a normal huntsman and you did not just trip and fall face-first on your own spear'

WHAT YOUR FAVOURITE WEAPON SAYS ABOUT YOU

FISTS

You've been around a long time and there's not much you haven't seen. While others come and go, you're always a loyal friend and can be counted upon in times of great need.

LONGBOW

You can be a little bit distant sometimes, but that's just how you operate. It takes a special person to be able to handle you, but you're not afraid to go the distance for them if need be.

SWORD

You're stylish and iconic, but you've still got a core of steel and can give as good as you get. You've got a sharp tongue that can hurt people if they're not careful, but those who don't get on your bad side have nothing to fear.

FLAIL

You've got a flare for the dramatic and aren't always the most practical person around. Although you can be a bit all over the place, people love having you around because you know how to put on a show.

GUN

You're a real trend-setter who's often ahead of the curve. Although your inner workings can be a bit of a mystery, people know you can be trusted to deliver good results.

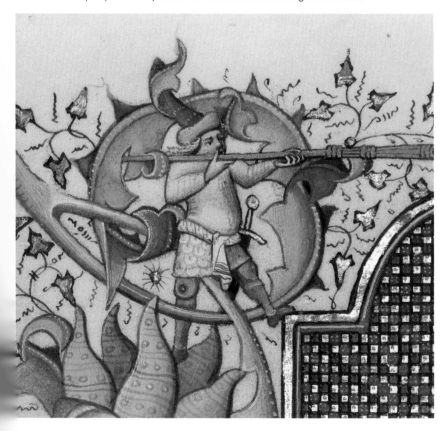

OBITUARIES: WEIRDEST DEATHS

Martin, King of Aragon, tragically passed in 1410 after his jester told him a joke so funny, he laughed himself to death. We are told that he died doing what he loved, if that provides any comfort to the bereaved. For safety reasons, the joke will not be repeated here.

We are saddened to announce the death of Basil I, Byzantine Emperor, who in 886 got his belt tangled in the antlers of a deer. The deer dragged poor Basil 16 miles through the woods and he did not survive the ordeal. The deer appears to be unharmed.

Richard the Raker, who worked emptying latrines in London, accidentally fell into a cesspit full of sewage and drowned in 1326. He is survived by his son, Sam the Smelly, who reportedly works in the same profession as his father.

The beloved Crown Prince Philip of France was taken from us before his time while riding his horse through Paris in 1131. A pig that ran out from a dung heap caused his steed to trip, and Philip's head did not find the Parisian cobblestones agreeable.

Gone but not forgotten, Pope Adrian IV's glorious life was brought to an abrupt end in 1159 while he drank water from a fountain. A fly that had been in the water became lodged in his throat and choked the poor man to death.

HOW WILL YOU DIE?

Now this is exciting! It's time to find out what's going to do you in. I don't want to hear any complaints from you about dying, okay? You know, most people don't get to find out this information until the last minute. Answer honestly, tally up the letters and prepare yourself for your fate.

Do you often enter into fights or arguments?
A. Yes, and I always win because of my superior intellectual and physical prowess
B. No, for I am meek and am cursed with a delicate constitution
C. Sometimes, but only if my opponent is weak and will easily be subjugated

What is your greatest fear?
A. Dying before my acts of valour and bravery are recorded in an epic ballad to be sung for centuries afterwards
B. Treacherous deeds from my enemies, because I have a lot of enemies and they are all very treacherous
C. Losing my vast hoard of wealth, which I have worked very hard to acquire

Imagine that you are at a grand banquet with much food and fine wines. You notice that a lower-ranking lord has taken all of the salt for himself, leaving none for you. What do you do?
A. I draw my sword and inform him loudly that he is my inferior and I wish to duel him to the death
B. I did not actually want salt on my food anyway so it's completely fine and I do not wish to pursue the matter further
C. I do not say anything, but after the meal has concluded I seduce his wife as an act of vengeance

What behaviour is sure to get someone uninvited from your hunting parties?
A. Cowardice in the face of danger
B. Coarse and unpleasant speech
C. Lacking the ability to joke and jest

How frequently do you venture beyond the walls of your city?
A. I have travelled far and wide and brought back many tales of distant lands
B. Rarely, as I have everything I need in my home
C. I am a bit of a vagabond and rarely settle in one place for long

Now tally up those answers!

If you got mostly ...

A: You will die IN BATTLE. Hey, at least you went down fighting!

B: You will die of DISEASE. Don't feel too bad, there was nothing you could do!

C: You commited too many crimes and will die IN PRISON. You rascal!

HOW TO CRUSADE

Reconquering the Holy Land in the name of the Lord is a fun and enriching activity for members of all social classes. Whether it's undertrained peasants or swaggering noblemen, you won't be able to tear them away from the walls of Jerusalem! Families and kids will love it, too. Here's everything you need.

INGREDIENTS:

* Equal measures of oppression and hardship (any type of hardship will do in a pinch, but this will work best if you can find some that has at least a little disease in it)
* A pinch of famine
* An entire continent's worth of sin and religious guilt
* A disenfranchised working class in Europe
* A new anti-Christian empire
* One Pope
* An impending apocalypse (here's a tip: if you can't find a real apocalypse in the shops, false rumours of an imaginary apocalypse will work just as well)

TIME:

Approximately three years (plus ten years for preparation)

YIELD:

Four Crusader states

> **Your Crusader states should last for a few decades if you give them enough supplies and troops.**

METHOD

1. At least ten years before you start, add the oppression, hardship and famine to the disenfranchised European working class. Mix well and sprinkle the sin and religious guilt on top, but reserve a pinch for later. As you do this, you'll notice the beginnings of unrest start to brew among the working class. Set aside for at least ten years to allow the unrest to build up further. This takes a while but do not skip this step!

2. In the meantime, introduce your new anti-Christian empire to Turkey. It will spread across the Middle East and Central Asia and eventually reach the Holy Land, where it should capture Jersalem from the Byzantine Empire. If you've used a good-quality empire with a high level of religious intolerance, you'll notice oppression and expulsion of Christians and Jews begin to occur.

3. Introduce the Pope to the scenario. He wants to reclaim the Holy Land and he'll be quick to promise the working class that they will be forgiven of all of their sins if they help him. He's the Pope, he can do that. If you added enough sin and religious guilt in the beginning, the peasants will be extremely enticed by this prospect.

4. Now you need to act quickly! While the peasants are excited by the idea of a permanent, all-expenses-paid stay in Heaven, dump the impending apocalypse into the mix. Even if it's not a real apocalypse, the rumours that it is real will be all the peasants need to take up arms and march for Jerusalem. Don't want to burn in Hell when Armageddon comes, do they?

5. Congratulations, now you have a Crusade! Sit back and let those zealous farmers try to take Jerusalem back for good, and enjoy watching them establish several unstable Crusader states in the Middle East.

UNDER SIEGE

We've all been there before: your enemies are occupying a strategically advantageous position, sequestered behind tall stone walls in a city well equipped with defensive weaponry and provisions. You've tried to breach their defences with all the usual tactics like catapults and flaming arrows, and nothing has worked. But you want to capture their stronghold so badly! It's a classic conundrum.

Here are a few creative siege solutions from medieval tacticians.

Bird
Any bird will do, but ideally one you're not too emotionally attached to

Enemy City
Should be close enough that the bird can reach it before it explodes

Cat
In case the bird gets lost on the way

Explosives
Don't forget this step

Enemy firepower
Try not to think too much about that

Unsuspecting fools
They think they're safe

Catapult
It's the bread and butter of sieging

'Impassable' moat
About to get passed

Your most aerodynamic soldier
Failing that, your most gullible

'Oh no, they brought the exploding cats. It's over'

DEATH
WITH DIGNITY

There are worse things than dying in battle, you know.
In fact, it's rather glamourous to go down swinging.
Think about how noble and dramatic you'll look
as you take a crossbow bolt to the face! Songs will
be sung about your heroic demise for years to
come, probably. Doesn't sound so bad, does it?
If you can't get excited to die, aim for ambivalence at
the very least. To get you inspired, here are a few brave
souls who feel pretty okay about their violent ends.

**Guess I'll die,
Germany, 15th century**

**A stabbing,
Switzerland,
14th century**

'Honestly, I wasn't even paying attention'

Flash your killers the
ol' finger guns to let them know
you won't take it personally

Strike a pose,
Netherlands,
15th century

UNCIVIL DISPUTES

Oops, you crossed the wrong person. Maybe you seduced their spouse or plotted to kill them or maybe they just hate you. Whichever it is, they've taken the matter to the authorities, which means you've just become embroiled in a fierce legal battle. How can you assert your innocence to the court? You're going to have to fight for it. Trial by combat, baby.

If you are both of the same gender, you can just hack each other to bits the good old-fashioned way. The person who slaughters the other is obviously innocent. But if a man and a woman are to face each other in combat, we'll need to level the playing field a bit.

The German fencing master Hans Talhoffer came up with an innovative solution to the issue. Here's what he suggests:

The man is placed in a hole up to his waist and is not allowed to leave for the duration of the fight. He is given a club to use as his weapon.

The woman stands on the ground above the hole and can move around as she wishes. Her weapon is a big rock in a cloth bag.

Simple enough, right? Here are a few techniques to look out for if you ever find yourself in such a duel.

Just guys doing guy stuff, France, 15th century

89

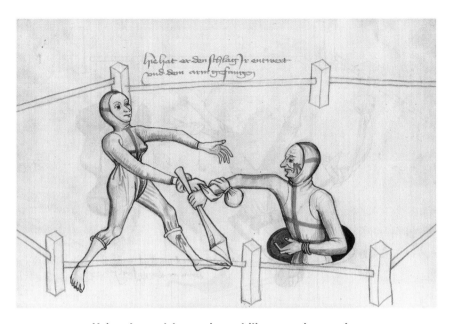

Using the rock bag to immobilise: very innovative

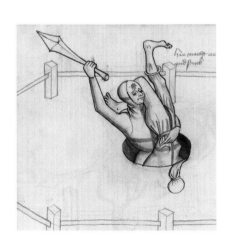

**The man catches her
with a piledriver:
victory goes to him**

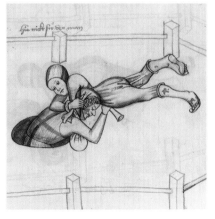

**The woman gets him
in a stranglehold:
victory goes to her**

WHAT IS YOUR PUNISHMENT?

The verdict is in and you're guilty as charged.
Before you can be sentenced, we will have to assess
how much of a danger you pose to society. The questions
on this page will test your knowledge of real laws and court
cases. The more you answer correctly, the less severe your
punishment will be. Answer too many wrong and you'll be
regretting your criminal ways very soon!

1. Say you fancy a game of foot ball with your pals. Under what circumstances would this be illegal? (*England, 1349*)

A. If you're playing on public land
B. On Sundays and other Church holidays
C. If women are playing
D. It's always illegal

2. A new neighbour moves in next door with his wife, who's quite the looker. She takes an interest in you and proposes the two of you start an affair.

What is one thing that may happen if you guys get caught? (*England, 7th century*)

A. They'll chop off your head
B. You'll enter into a duel with your neighbour for her hand
C. You'll be held responsible for finding your neighbour a new wife
D. You'll both be branded with symbols of shame for all to see

3. One of your pigs gets loose from its pen and happens to kill a small child while roaming the streets. Who will be held accountable for this by the courts?
(*France, 1494*)

A. You
B. The child
C. The pig
D. The child's family

4. Which of the following has *never* been a valid reason to divorce your husband?
(*Ireland, c. 8th century*)

A. He gossips about your intimate life
B. He bathes less than twice a month
C. You don't like his concubine
D. He engages in homosexual acts

5. What crime was nobleman Salvagio de Aste caught committing on at least seven different occasions?
(*Italy, 16th century*)

A. Stealing sausages from the butcher
B. Wearing clothes that were too fancy
C. Refusing to take off his hat in church
D. Blaspheming against the Pope

0 correct: Off with your head!

1–2 correct: Ten years in prison.

3–4 correct: Three days in the stocks. You'll probably be fine, but your feet will be exposed for passersby to tickle, slap and otherwise abuse. A lot can happen to feet in three days, you know.

5 correct: You escaped from prison! You hit the road and are never seen again.

Now, add up the number of questions you got correct and read on to learn your fate:

1. A 2. C
3. C
4. B 5. B

EUROPE'S MOST WANTED

Now that you've turned to a life of crime, there's probably no going back, even if you do make it out of prison somehow. So why not double down and commit some even bigger crimes when you get the chance? If you need any ideas, here are a few notorious outlaws whose misdeeds earned them fame far and wide.

Judge, jury and executioner

JOHN PENROS: Frenemy of the Law

John was a talented lawyer who quickly ascended to the position of Lord Chief Justice of Ireland. Perhaps sick of enforcing the rules, he decided to start breaking them instead, and soon faced accusations of burglary, treason and murder. This didn't stop John: he kept practising as a lawyer and as a criminal for years afterwards, and never saw any punishment for his deeds.

Every pirate has to start somewhere

JEANNE DE CLISSON:
Lioness of Brittany

After the French king wrongfully executed her husband for treason, Jeanne swore she would have her revenge. She raised a force of 400 men and bought three warships, painting them black and dying the sails red. For thirteen years, Jeanne hunted French ships and decimated their crews, and she always made sure that a few sailors were left alive to tell the king who had slaughtered his men. Though she settled back down on dry land eventually, her career as a corsair was not in vain: with the English support she'd won, Jeanne secured herself a barony, a castle, another husband and a long life in peace.

EUSTACE THE MONK:
Unholy Man

To his peers, Eustace seemed like just another monk, but legend has it he was secretly the most powerful wielder of black magic in France. We'll never know if he really made a deal with the devil, but for some reason Eustace decided one day to turn to a life of piracy. He sold out to the English as a mercenary, then betrayed them to the French, wreaking havoc across the English Channel for over a decade before he was caught and beheaded.

When good monks go bad

DIVINE
HEALING

So, your standard cures didn't work? Plague buboes won't disappear? Don't worry, there's a pretty fail-safe option for these situations: get down on your knees and start praying. If God Himself can't answer your plea, there's probably a saint or two with a free minute to help you out. Using their divine power, they'll set you straight right away. Don't believe it? Here are some times that the divine have intervened.

This probably could have been prevented by better axe-safety skills, but that's beside the point. A severed leg is nothing compared to the Virgin Mary's healing powers

Mary's miracles don't stop there: she cured a man of mouth cancer with nothing more than a kiss! The angel was there to make sure the encounter didn't progress any further

A quiet dinner at the abbey almost turned sour when a nun started to choke on a bone. Thankfully, St Hedwig was on the scene and pulled the offending article out of her trachea with a mere gesture and a benevolent smile

Louis IX was said to channel divine healing powers through his intense faith. Here he is pictured curing a man of scrofula. If you ever start to feel scrofulous, call Louis IX to banish your scrofulosis for good!

JUDGEMENT DAY

Wait, you didn't think that it just all ended when you died, right? The whole point of life is to figure out what's going to happen afterwards. If you were good, you'll be rewarded most handsomely, and if you were bad, well, let's not think about that just yet. It's time for your soul to be judged and your eternal fate to be decided.

Were you ever angry?
A. I have complete control over my emotions
B. Sometimes I yell a little bit when I'm upset
C. I'm angry at absolutely everything all of the time

Did you go to church when you were supposed to?
A. I went even when I wasn't supposed to
B. I forgot to go a couple of times, but I would have loved to have been there
C. I've never even set foot in that stupid place

Did you use profanity?
A. I would never denigrate my mouth with foul language
B. What's a little bit of swearing among friends?
C. I utter shocking obscenities every time I open my goddamn mouth

Did you stay true to your faith in God?
A. I have never forsaken the light of the Lord
B. I struggled with my faith sometimes, but I'm pretty sure God is real
C. God is dead and I killed him

**Have you ever taken
something that wasn't yours?**
A. No, I want not for material wealth
B. I almost always successfully
resisted the urge to steal
C. I'm stealing right now

**Have you ever
murdered someone?**
A. I'm offended that you
would even ask
B. No, but if my idiot
brother-in-law
got murdered I wouldn't
complain
C. My hands are soaked
in the blood of innocents

**Have you repented
for your sins?**
A. I have done all that
I can to make amends
B. I feel really bad about them,
but I never got around to doing
a proper penance
C. My only regret is that
I couldn't sin more

Mostly A: Congratulations, you made it into HEAVEN! You were a good person and didn't sin too much, and if you did you probably felt really bad about it. Your soul will now be carried up to the clouds by a fleet of angels, where you will experience eternal and perfect happiness. Some famous people who went to Heaven include: King Solomon, Thomas Aquinas and Jesus.

Mostly B: Looks like you're going to PURGATORY! You probably sinned a little bit but nothing too major. Your soul can still be saved, but first you're going to be punished to pay off your sin debt. Eventually, angels will come and carry you to Heaven. Just keep praying and you'll get through it! Some famous people who went to purgatory include: King Henry III of England and Pope Adrian V.

Mostly C: Oops, straight to HELL! You probably loved sinning and your life was an affront to God. You cannot be saved and will burn for ever. Demons will spend every day inventing new and gruesome ways to torment you. Some famous people who went to Hell include: Attila the Hun, Judas Iscariot and Satan.

Going to heaven, Flanders, *c.* 1500

Going to hell, Flanders, *c.* 1500

Christ's side wound, Luxembourg, 14th century

PART 2

THE
BESTIARY

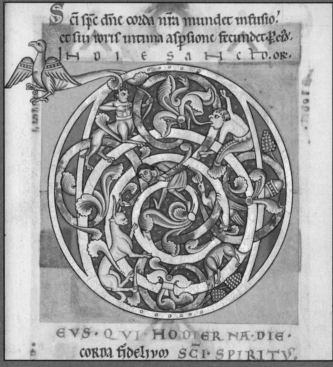

BEASTS
Creatures That Walk the Earth

FISH
Creatures That Swim the Seas

BIRDS
Creatures That Fly the Heavens

SERPENTS
Creatures That Slither and Crawl

Just like humans, animals may be good, evil, or somewhere in between. But while a person usually lets you know which of those they are as soon as they open their mouth, an animal can be harder to figure out. You might not think it's worth it to ponder the morality of snails and hedgehogs, but I can assure you that God disagrees. He put all those creatures on the Earth with us for a reason, didn't He? In some cases, it was to be useful: to provide humans with food, companionship or unpaid labour. Some animals are even very wise, wiser perhaps than some people. But many of these animals serve as cautionary tales; they are harbingers of villainy, sin and danger. These should be avoided like the devil.

The bestiary is your handy who's who of the animal kingdom, written to spare you the trouble of figuring out on your own how each one should be treated. Is it a good idea to eat an owl? Are wolves friendly and gentle souls? Are fish better parents than bears? All the questions that have been plaguing you are answered within. I know you're excited to wander into the wild world out there, but before you go I suggest you take a look through the following pages and familiarise yourself with the characters you may meet along the way.

> **Then God said, 'Let us make mankind in our image, in our likeness, so that they may rule over the fish in the sea and the birds in the sky, over the livestock and all the wild animals, and over all the creatures that move along the ground.'**

GENESIS 1:26

BEASTS

CREATURES THAT WALK THE EARTH

As I am sure you already know, there are four categories of animal in the world: beasts, birds, fish and serpents. Every creature can be placed into one of those groups. If you think you know of an animal that's not a beast, bird, fish or serpent, you're wrong. God created those categories. They're true. The bestiary will present animals to you in these categories, too.

We're going to start off with beasts because they're a very special category. These are the creatures with fur and fang that walk the Earth alongside us. Our closest companions, our beasts of burden, and our nearest kin. Who could look into the eyes of a hound and fail to see a little bit of humanity looking back? Who could deny the benevolence of the noble lion, who surely would never kill humans for sport? Not all beasts are friendly, of course: among  this group are some of the deadliest, most cunning animals on Earth. Some of them, like the cat, even walk among humans, concealing their true nature. You'll need to be just as strong and clever if you want to avoid the dangers of the beasts.

THE LION

LATIN NAME: LEO

WHERE IT ABIDES: LORDING OVER ITS KINGDOM AND ALL THE LOWLY BEINGS WITHIN IT

STRENGTHS: KILLER HAIR, AN ALMOST ANTHROPOMORPHIC SENSE OF JUSTICE

WEAKNESSES: FEAR OF ROOSTERS, FEAR OF BEING FOUND OUT AS A ROOSTER-FEARER

VIRTUE: 5 ✳ **BEAUTY**: 5 ✳ **DANGER**: 4

The lion is the vainest by far of all animals, and because of that a group of lions is called a pride. This fearsome feline is noble, virtuous, and kills any creature that refuses to yield to its might, which is how it has earned the esteemed title of 'king of the beasts'. Luckily, your chances of stumbling across a lion on your way to the market or out in the turnip fields are pretty low, but it's a good idea to practise bowing and scraping just in case. If the lion is convinced by your act, it will almost definitely probably not slice you into rib-bons. Assuming you make it out, learn from the lion: next time *you* are about to commit an act of senseless violence against a helpless victim, give them a chance to surrender before you go in for the kill. It's the noble thing to do.

No animal dares defy the lion. No animal except one, that is – the lion is terrified of the rooster and will cower and tremble in fear if it sees one. Lions don't want you to know that, so try not to tell them you heard it from me – it's not the best PR for the so-called king of the beasts.

In the top drawing, we see the regal lion showing mercy to men who bow down to its glory. Below, the lion bows before a rooster, hoping for a similar act of goodwill. The rooster seems to still be thinking it over

THE WOLF

LATIN NAME: LUPUS

WHERE IT ABIDES: DEEP IN THE DARKEST WOODS, WAITING FOR ERRANT TRAVELLERS TO CROSS ITS PATH

STRENGTHS: NOT MUCH OF A FUSSY EATER

WEAKNESSES: PRUDISH, CAN'T HANDLE BEING LOOKED AT

VIRTUE: 1 ✳ **BEAUTY:** 1 ✳ **DANGER:** 4

The wolf is a truly wicked creature. Anything it sees, it will pounce on, and anything it pounces on, it will eat. But you will not often see the wolf, because much like the devil, it is a coward and would rather hide in darkness than show its face by light of day. Because this beast is so dangerous, it is very valuable to know what to do if you encounter one in the wild. Here are a few dos and don'ts that will help any honest soul fend off a wolf:

1. DO make sure you see the wolf before the wolf sees you. If you look at the wolf first, it will lose its courage and no longer attack. Then, when it is helpless, you can bite it.

2. DO NOT let the wolf see you first. If this happens, you will be struck dumb, leaving you unable to cry for help. Then, when you are helpless, the wolf will bite you. That monster.

3. DO take your clothes off. Yes, that's right. If, by some chance, that tricky wolf caught you off guard and saw you first, there's still hope. You need to strip down to your underwear, grab two rocks, and start banging them together as hard as you can. Seeing this, the wolf will turn tail and run. (This also works on creepy men, tax collectors and in-laws.)

4. DO NOT feel bad about killing the wolf. The wolf wants you to feel bad about killing it. It's a classic wolf trick. Wolves are not protected by the law. There are no legal repercussions for killing a wolf.

THE HEDGEHOG

LATIN NAME: ERICIUS

WHERE IT ABIDES: IN BURROWS DEEP INSIDE TANGLY THICKETS, WHERE NO CREATURE CAN DISTURB IT

STRENGTHS: MASTER OF SELF-DEFENCE, NO NEED FOR SHOPPING BAGS

WEAKNESSES: AVOIDANT OF CONFRONTATION

VIRTUE: 3 ✳ **BEAUTY:** 2 ✳ **DANGER:** 2

The hedgehog is a little creature, tremendously rotund and covered head to toe in bristly spines with which it is able to defend against many dangers. It uses a very cunning tactic: when it senses a threat, the hedgehog lays on the ground and curls into a ball with its sharp quills pointing out in every direction and quietly hopes the issue will resolve itself.[1]

When the hedgehog goes out in search of food, it climbs up into orchard trees and grapevines to knock fruit down to the ground. Then, the hedgehog rolls over the fruit so that it is all impaled upon its spikes, and this way is able to carry a great amount of food back to its home.

---

1. Many humans do this, too, just without the quills.

'My favourite food is actually steak, but it's a lot harder to impale a cow on your spikes than it is a grape'[2]

Extremely rotund hedgehog, Italy, 15th century

---

2. Artistic depictions of the hedgehog with fruit upon its spines were extremely popular in medieval bestiaries and can be found in modern media even today, primarily in storybooks and animations for children. It seems that the image of the spiny little urchin carrying apples home to its family has retained its appeal over the centuries. And maybe one day we'll even catch them doing it!

THE UNICORN

ofperit de excello sancto suo:
s de celo in terra aspent:
iret gemitus compedtorii:
t filios interemptorium:

LATIN NAME: UNICORNIS

WHERE IT ABIDES: WHEREVER THE PRYING EYES OF GREEDY POACHERS CAN'T REACH

STRENGTHS: BEAUTIFUL, PERFECT, ANGELIC, WONDERFUL

WEAKNESSES: NOT THAT SMART

VIRTUE: 5 ✳ **BEAUTY**: 5 ✳ **DANGER**: 2

The unicorn is a reclusive creature. It is said to be the most majestic of animals, full of grace and nobility, the sweetest and most pure-hearted thing you will ever set your eyes on. Those who have report that it is very small, fluffy, and has four legs with hooves and a solitary horn projecting from the centre of its head. The horn is extremely valuable for its many medicinal properties, as it can act as an antivenom, a cure for fatal diseases and as an aphrodisiac. Because of its power, a full unicorn horn can cost as much as a castle, which is a lot.[1]

Of course, if it was easy to hunt a unicorn for its horn, every peasant and their dog would have one. In fact, these horns are also extremely rare because unicorns are too swift and strong to be caught by hunters. However, there is *one* way to snare one.

In order to catch a unicorn, you must find a virgin girl and lead her to a forest where unicorns dwell. Seeing the girl, the unicorn will be drawn to her and soon rest its head upon her lap and fall asleep.

---

1. The long, spiral horns that were sold to medieval Europeans were most often tusks from narwhals hunted in the North Atlantic. How these came to be labelled as extremely expensive 'unicorn horns' is anyone's guess …

At this point, you can jump out of the bushes where you were hiding (you remembered to hide in the bushes, right?), stab the noble, rare beast to death, and slice off its horn. There's your rent for the next 500 years!

A girls' night out goes badly awry, Flanders, 13th century

THE FOX

LATIN NAME: VULPIS

WHERE IT ABIDES: IN CLOSE PROXIMITY TO CHICKEN COOPS, TRYING HARD NOT TO LOOK SUSPICIOUS

STRENGTHS: KNACK FOR ACTING, COULD MAKE IT BIG IN SHOWBIZ

WEAKNESSES: ENEMY OF THE LAW

VIRTUE: 1 ✷ **BEAUTY:** 2 ✷ **DANGER:** 2

The fox is crafty to its core and will never meet a problem head-on, preferring always to use trickery and deception. A fine example of this is the fox's favourite way to hunt. Noble beasts like the lion pursue their prey until it collapses or overwhelm it with great strength, as God intended. However, a hungry fox will set about finding a patch of red mud and roll around in it until its fur looks bloody. Then, it simply walks into a field and lies down belly-up, pretending to be dead. It is never long before an unsuspecting bird spots the fox and flies closer to investigate, at which point it very quickly becomes bones.

Foxes appear in many a fable as trickster characters because of their wily nature. There is no better example of this than Reynard the Fox, the quintessential troublemaker of many folk tales. Reynard is known as a scourge throughout the forest, where the other animals are perpetual victims of his trickery. They spend most of the story trying to bring Reynard to justice for various crimes, including:

1. Killing and eating the children of Chanticleer the rooster
2. Pretending to be a priest so he could kill and eat other animals more easily
3. Seducing the wife of King Noble the lion

Trickery, England, 14th century

Justice, England, 14th century

THE CAT

LATIN NAME: CATUS

WHERE IT ABIDES: NEVER FAR FROM A SNACK

STRENGTHS: HIGHLY DECEPTIVE, DISARMINGLY FUZZY

WEAKNESSES: DOGS SEE RIGHT THROUGH ITS NONSENSE

VIRTUE: 2 ✳ **BEAUTY:** 2 ✳ **DANGER:** 5

The cat is the most dangerous beast of them all. Yes, it may appear to be a useful creature in your household, with its keen senses and propensity for sudden outbursts of violence towards rats and mice. It may even charm and beguile you with its gentle purring and angelic appearance. Yet, if you are so foolish as to let a cat into your home, you will find out the very opposite is true.

The cat can *never* be tamed! It will however, tame *you*.[1]

It is crucial that you do not allow yourself to be taken in by the cat's wiles, no matter how much it tries to win you over. So that you don't fall victim in the future, please familiarise yourself with these classic cat tactics which it uses to trick honest humans into giving it shelter.

---

1. Cats may be some of the most controversial animals of all time. Their association with witchcraft and devilry stretches back to the Middle Ages, and in medieval Flanders and France it is said that cats were frequently killed en masse. Things weren't so bad everywhere, though. There are records of cat shelters existing in the Middle East before 1500, and one Persian manuscript from 600 tells us that 'women kept cats as pets, dying their fur, adorning them with jewellery, and letting them sleep in their beds'.

Musical hypnosis
Cat playing the organ, Flanders,
15th century

**Disguising itself
as a snail**
Snail cat, France,
15th century

**Pretending to help with
household chores**
Cat churning butter,
Flanders or Germany, c. 1300

THE BEAR

*θυλοκρ δεγορως, μηδεσγμβασηςνο(6
φαζαντπαν κράλιςε ζᵈ χυκοκλονον • +
Σμλος.*

LATIN NAME: URSUS[1]

WHERE IT ABIDES: IN DEEP, DARK CAVES, WHERE NO SENSIBLE PERSON WOULD VENTURE

STRENGTHS: EXPERT IN CHILD DEVELOPMENT

WEAKNESSES: HONEY ADDICT, WILL DO ANYTHING FOR ITS NEXT FIX

VIRTUE: 3 ✳ **BEAUTY:** 2 ✳ **DANGER:** 4

The bear is a mighty and fearsome beast, but it is also much like a human, for it can stand on two legs as few other beasts can. The female is pregnant for only 30 days, and because her gestation period is so short, the young that she births are simply featureless lumps of flesh. The mother bear then licks her blobs/cubs to carefully sculpt them into their proper shape. If you ever happen to see a bear cub that looks a bit off, its mother probably isn't too artistically inclined, but that's just the risk you run being a bear.

---

1. The Ancient Greek word for bear is *arktos*. Ancient Germanic tribes in the first millennium BCE used a similar word, *arkto*. However, a pervasive fear that saying the true name of the creature would cause bears to physically appear led speakers to replace *arkto* with a euphemism, *bera*, likely meaning either 'brown one' or 'wild animal'. It is from *bera* that the modern English *bear* evolved.

'Just a little snack before bed'

BEWARE THE BEARS

The Bible tells us the story of Elisha,
a prophet who was taunted by a group
of boys who made fun of his bald spot.
The wise and just Elisha used his holy
powers to call two bears out of the woods
to devour the boys.

Let's hope that taught them a lesson!

THE MANTICORE

LATIN NAME: MANTICORA

WHERE IT ABIDES: WHEREVER HUMAN FLESH CAN BE FOUND - IF YOU'RE READING THIS, IT MIGHT BE NEAR BY

STRENGTHS: NATURE'S MOST PERFECT PREDATOR

WEAKNESSES: PLEASE LET US KNOW IF YOU FIND ANY

VIRTUE: 1 * **BEAUTY:** 1 * **DANGER:** 5

The manticore is a fearsome beast with the face of a man and the body of a lion. It has three rows of teeth, and upon the end of its tail is a stinger that transmits a most deadly poison. As soon as the stinger pierces your skin, you will begin to die in agony. Some have reported that it actually can shoot stingers in every direction, like arrows. The manticore is an extremely powerful hunter, capable of running fast and leaping great distances to pursue its prey. Its favourite meal is human flesh, but it will settle for any other type of raw flesh in a pinch.

The manticore allegedly makes a noise that sounds like a cross between reed pipes and trumpets, so at least you get to hear some nice music before you die in agony, I guess? It's hard to find a positive take on this thing.

A rather less well-known trait of the manticore is its love of funny hats,
which it often wears while stalking and devouring its prey

THE DOG

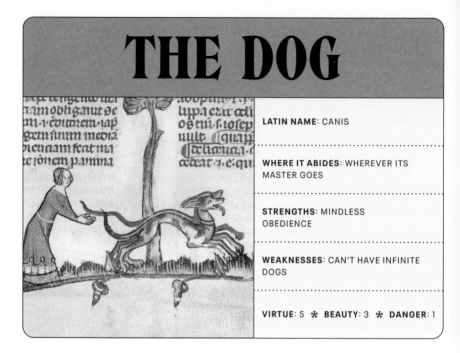

LATIN NAME: CANIS

WHERE IT ABIDES: WHEREVER ITS MASTER GOES

STRENGTHS: MINDLESS OBEDIENCE

WEAKNESSES: CAN'T HAVE INFINITE DOGS

VIRTUE: 5 ✳ **BEAUTY:** 3 ✳ **DANGER:** 1

The dog is a very wise creature, for it is the only creature that recognises its own name! (Present company excluded.) The value of a person is indicated by whether they love and value dogs, and the care they take in training them and treating them well. In return for your care, your dog is certain to be your faithful companion for life. And perhaps even after that: it is well known that when a dog's master has been murdered, the dog is able to recognise the killer on sight and will not cease to snap and bark at the scoundrel until he has been apprehended. Keep a dog in your home, if not for your own benefit now, then for the hypothetical benefit of swift justice in the event that you're one day murdered.

The more dogs you have, the better person you are, so you'll want to get a lot of dogs. You may struggle to think of suitable names for your vast arsenal of hounds. Luckily, an English nobleman by the name of Edward, Duke of York, once wrote out a list of 1,126 names he found to be appropriate for all manner of dogs.

Here is a brief excerpt:

Nosewise
Stykefaste
Garlik
Grimbolde
Bonyfaunte
Strawnge
Pretyman
Snacke
Norman
Filthe

EVERYONE NEEDS A DOG

There are characters of all kinds on these pages,
both noble and humble, good and evil.
They have one thing in common, though:
every single one of them has a dog!

**King John
loved his dogs**

**A lady needs a dog,
of course – how else is
she to hunt?**

**Pontius Pilate?
He had a dog, too, apparently**

THE CENTAUR

LATIN NAME: CENTAURUS

WHERE IT ABIDES: SOME SAY THAT CENTAURS LIVE SOMEWHERE IN AFRICA (YOU KNOW, THAT FARAWAY COUNTRY)

STRENGTHS: KNOWS HOW TO PARTY

WEAKNESSES: DOESN'T KNOW HOW TO STOP PARTYING

VIRTUE: 1 ✳ **BEAUTY:** 2 ✳ **DANGER:** 2

The centaur is a brutish beast with the upper body of a man and the lower body of a horse[1]. They love to hunt, drink to excess and revel in their herds. They may be as intelligent as humans, but they are also as wild, lustful and hedonistic as horses. They represent an important message, for within all of us dwells a little bit of rational human but also a little bit of horny horse; our inner human and inner horse are forever destined to battle each other for dominance. Be wary that you do not let the horse win, lest you fall eternally into sin and drunkenness. As horses are known to do.

> **That moustache just screams 'freak', doesn't it?**

---

1. Although the horse part is actually an entire horse except for the head and neck. Technically, this means that centaurs have two hearts, four nipples and 60 ribs. Just something to think about.

If centaurs were really half man and half horse, this is what they would look like

'I'm actually half centaur and half horse, which is why I was born without arms'

THE ELEPHANT

LATIN NAME: ELEPHAS

WHERE IT ABIDES: IN GREAT HERDS THAT LUMBER ACROSS THE FIELDS LIKE MOVING MOUNTAIN RANGES

STRENGTHS: ENORMOUS MUSCLES, ENORMOUS RESERVES OF ALTRUISM

WEAKNESSES: CAN'T STAND UP

VIRTUE: 5 ✳ **BEAUTY:** 2 ✳ **DANGER:** 3

The elephant is a creature the size of a mountain, with two ivory tusks and a nose that looks like a snake. Whatever object the elephant wraps its proboscis around or treads underfoot is crushed to bits by its size and strength. You will be happy to hear, then, that the elephant is a good and noble creature and a friend to all humans. Despite its great size and strength, it never intentionally causes harm, and if it does accidentally stomp someone to death, it always feels very sorry about it. However, the elephant has one primary weakness, which is that it has no knees, and because of this cannot stand back up if it falls.[1]

If these gentle giants come across a person lost in the desert, elephants will do all they can to lead the wayward soul back to safety.

---

1. This is a myth: elephants do have knees. Another popular myth claims that elephants in fact have *four* knees, twice as many as other land mammals. This is also untrue. Elephants have two knees. The normal amount of knees.

Elephants at war, England, 13th century

Elephants at peace, England, 13th century

BIRDS

CREATURES THAT FLY THE HEAVENS

Every creature that flies is, by definition, a bird. As far as good symbols go, the bird has always been a front-runner, and it's not necessarily hard to see why. To begin with, birds live in the sky, which is where Heaven is, which is where God is. God wouldn't have let them up there if He didn't like them. A lot of birds sing beautiful songs to entertain us humans, which is very thoughtful of them, so they must be rather nice creatures on the whole. And most birds stay out of the dirt and eat nice things like fruit and grains, which is sure evidence of civility.

Of course, not all birds hold themselves to the same high standards. Some, like the bat and the owl, seem to have abandoned the proper bird lifestyle and instead fly around by night, hiding from God's light, and make awful screeching noises, and wallow about in filth. Why they have chosen to be such nasty creatures is anyone's guess, but it's a sure sign they're meant to be avoided.

THE EAGLE

LATIN NAME: AQUILA

WHERE IT ABIDES: IN NESTS ON TREACHEROUS CLIFFS OVERLOOKING THE SEA

STRENGTHS: HIGH FLIER

WEAKNESSES: DEMANDING PARENT

VIRTUE: 5 ✳ **BEAUTY:** 5 ✳ **DANGER:** 2

The eagle is a most noble and special bird for several reasons, the principal of these being that it lives for ever. Eventually, over the course of its long life, the eagle gets very old and withered and gradually begins to go blind. This, of course, happens to the best of us mortals. But the eagle has a solution. It flies up to the sun and its old feathers are burnt off. At this point it resembles a (very regal) plucked chicken. Then, it plunges down to the ocean and the seawater washes the mist off its eyes, and the eagle is once again like a young bird.

Eagles have very powerful sight, and it is said that they can stare directly into the sun. However, not all baby eagles are born with this ability. In order to root these out, the mother eagle forces all of her chicks to stare directly into the sun. Those that look away are promptly chucked out of the nest. In some cultures this is known as child abuse, but to eagles it's just basic pedagogy.

Dante tells us in his poem 'Paradise' that the souls of the just in Heaven join together in the form of a massive, radiant eagle. If you, reader, wish to join the giant soul eagle in the sky and chat with famous world leaders, you had best live a moral and upright life. The eagle doesn't accept just anyone, you know. It's a very exclusive bird.

Uultur a uolatu tardo nominatur. Magnitu
dine quippe corporis precipites uolatus non
habet. Vultures dicuntur non misceri concubitu: et

'I don't want this either, kids, but your brother Tommy is weak'

'Sorry, the eagle is full right now. If you repent for your sins and live a pious life, we might be able to squeeze you in next Tuesday'

THE SIREN

LATIN NAME: SIRENA

WHERE IT ABIDES: ON CRAGGY ROCKS IN STORM-TOSSED OCEANS

STRENGTHS: TALENTED SONGSTRESS, ALWAYS HAS A CAPTIVE AUDIENCE

WEAKNESSES: CAN'T KEEP A BOYFRIEND FOR LONG

VIRTUE: 1 ✳ **BEAUTY:** 5 ✳ **DANGER:** 4

The siren appears as a woman from the waist up, but her lower half is that of a wretched bird. These half-women have beautiful faces and sing sweetly to sailors as their ships pass by the ocean rocks where sirens roost. So enchanting is their music, the sailors soon fall fast asleep, and the sirens pounce upon them and tear them to shreds. Not to eat or anything, they just love shredding sailors.

The bishop Leander of Seville wrote that all women are either nuns or sirens. To put his message more simply, women cannot be attractive *and* good. A beautiful woman is just a vicious siren waiting to tempt you into sin. No exceptions. Just as the only way to escape a siren is to plug your ears to block its song and sail away swiftly, if you see a pretty lady you should ignore her, turn and run. If you *are* a pretty lady, I'm sorry. There's no hope for you.

'Oh wow, you're a personification of the evils of human sexuality too? No wonder they keep drawing us together. We should hang out sometime!'

'Usually if the singing doesn't get them, a little horn solo does the trick'

THE BAT

LATIN NAME: VESPERTILIO

WHERE IT ABIDES: IN DARK CAVES AND TOMBS WHERE NO CLEAN CREATURE WOULD DARE DWELL

STRENGTHS: NIGHT VISION, WINGS ARE PRETTY COOL I GUESS

WEAKNESSES: KIND OF GROSS, A BIT WEIRD

VIRTUE: 1 ✳ **BEAUTY**: 1 ✳ **DANGER**: 1

The bat, like most creatures of the darkness, is not a proud beast. Although it is not particularly harmful, the bat is lowly and above all a filthy bird. It has wings of leather and dwells in only the darkest, dankest of crevasses where all the unsavoury types live. The other birds think the bat a very nasty little creature and keep away from it because they are greatly unnerved by its veiny, featherless wings and the strange movements it makes as it flutters across the (evening, always) sky.

Because anyone with a modicum of sense will follow this lead and keep their distance from the bat, it is difficult to know what a bat truly looks like.

This presents a tricky situation, because if we forget how to identify a bat, then it will become very difficult to avoid them in future. Therefore, the space below has been created to present to you the newest and most artistically advanced renderings of these creatures.

Our initial research suggests that bats are vulnerable to being bludgeoned with a tree branch. Provided our lady of the night doesn't misread this as a bouquet offering, this may be one way to successfully fend off a bat

It's actually possible that bats are very cute and we just haven't ever taken the time to check

THE SWAN

LATIN NAME: OLOR

WHERE IT ABIDES: ON PONDS OR STREAMS, WHERE IT MAY BE SEEN FLOATING ELEGANTLY ABOUT

STRENGTHS: MUSICALLY INCLINED

WEAKNESSES: WILL ENCOURAGE THEFT, JEALOUSY, INSECURITY AMONG YOUR RIVALS

VIRTUE: 1 ✳ **BEAUTY:** 2 ✳ **DANGER:** 2

The swan sings more sweetly than any other bird, and is said to sing its sweetest song when it knows it is about to die.[1] It is also more beautiful than any other bird on account of its white feathers and gracefully arched neck. Because the swan is such a perfect, special fowl, it must be protected from evil, and thus in England only the very wealthy are permitted by the king to own and eat swans. Therefore, you may recognise the worth of an Englishman by the number of swans he possesses. (Ladies, take heed: if a man courting you walks about covered in feathers with faint honking emitting from under his coat, then he must be very wealthy indeed.)

Each swan you buy will set you back around five shillings. This is approximately the annual wages for a household servant, but a swan will bring you far more joy than a cook or chambermaid, and can more easily be roasted and served at Christmas dinner.

---

1. Although many species of swan are known to sing, those native to Europe do not. The only noises they make are grunts, whistles and barks.

Swanning about, England, 13ᵗʰ century

THE PHOENIX

LATIN NAME: PHOENIX

WHERE IT ABIDES: IN THE HOT, DRY REGIONS OF ARABIA

STRENGTHS: ETERNAL LIFE

WEAKNESSES: TERMINALLY SINGLE

VIRTUE: 1 ✳ **BEAUTY**: 2 ✳ **DANGER**: 2

The phoenix is a bird with splendid plumage of brilliant red and gold and purple trailing from its body. It is a solitary bird, for there is only one phoenix in the whole world, but the phoenix doesn't mind that because it finds socialising to be a bit of a strain anyway. It ages very slowly and after 500 years of life builds a pyre in the topmost boughs of a tall tree. As the first rays of the rising sun shine upon the pyre, it bursts into flames, which the phoenix fans with its wings until itself and the pyre are reduced to ashes. Then, a new phoenix emerges from the ashes of the old, and it is another 500 years before the process repeats.

> 'In the most beautiful tree, over the most pleasant spring, it builds an altar like a nest of thyme and myrrh and cinnamon and precious spices.'
>
> –THOMAS OF CANTIMPRÉ

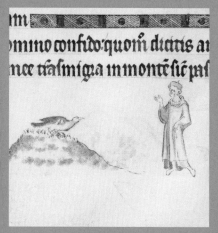

A solitary bird, here the phoenix shows that it would rather
be engulfed in flames than face a social interaction

'I'm not 500 yet, but I said something really embarrassing at a party
last night and I'm pretty sure everyone thinks I'm weird so I'm just going
to call it quits and light myself on fire right now'

THE BEE

LATIN NAME: APIS

WHERE IT ABIDES: IN GREAT BEEHIVES THAT THEY BUILD TOGETHER OUT OF BEESWAX

STRENGTHS: LAW-ABIDING, WELL-ORGANISED, HIGHLY MILITARISTIC

WEAKNESSES: GETS A LITTLE DEFENSIVE SOMETIMES

VIRTUE: 5 ✳ **BEAUTY:** 2 ✳ **DANGER:** 2

The bee, like the human, lives in an orderly society that abides by a fixed set of rules. Above all, bee society is governed by its monarch, the king[1] bee, who they exist to serve. They fiercely defend their hive in his honour and won't hesitate to die protecting it. Every bee has its role in the production of honey, and unlike your average human, they find joy in their work and certainly do not call in sick or say things like, 'I'm thinking about taking some time off to travel.' These little birds are truly role models for us all: next time you start wondering if there's more to life than milking cows and shovelling manure, act like a bee and stay in the dirt where you belong. Leave the important questions to the important people.

When bees feel that their hive has grown too crowded, some of their number will elect to leave home in search of a new place to stay. This is all well and good in nature, but if you consider yourself a beekeeper then it just won't do. In order to avoid becoming a bee*loser*, here is a simple charm you can recite to your bees that's sure to calm them down when they grow agitated:

---

1. Though nowadays it is well known that the leader of the beehive is a queen, most medieval authors describe the bees' monarch in strictly male terms. So much for girl power.

*Settle down, victory-women,
sink to earth,
never be wild and fly to the woods.*

*Be as mindful of my welfare,
as is each man of border
and of home.*

'Oh my god, Gilbert, I think this guy
forgot the bee charm'

Threats to the hive are destroyed by all means necessary

THE PELICAN

LATIN NAME: PELICANUS

WHERE IT ABIDES: WHEREVER ITS CHILDREN'S SCREAMS CAN'T BE HEARD

STRENGTHS: UNCONVENTIONAL PARENTING STRATEGIES

WEAKNESSES: STRAINED FAMILIAL RELATIONSHIPS

VIRTUE: 4 ✳ **BEAUTY**: 3 ✳ **DANGER**: 1

The pelican is a most noble bird and it is devoted above all to its children. The young pelicans, unfortunately, go through a bit of a difficult phase growing up and begin to strike out at their mother with their wings and beaks. In a fit of rage, the pelican pecks her children to death. This shuts the little monsters up, but soon the mother begins to feel horror at the cruelty of her deed. She lets the young lie dead in the nest for three days (she must not feel *that* much horror) and then pierces her own breast with her beak.[1] When the blood pours across the bodies of her children, they are brought back to life.

---

1. In addition to the long-beaked pelicans that exist in nature, some bestiaries describe a second, fictitious kind of pelican with a short beak, and this is the type usually depicted in their artwork. This is not unusual for bestiaries: owls and ostriches, for instance, are often drawn as generic birds resembling hawks or fowl. Considering the rather gawky appearance of the real pelican, which would probably struggle to pierce its own chest with its massive, blunt bill, some artistic liberties were perhaps necessary in order to align with the bestiaries' descriptions of a fierce, noble bird.

'Aw man, blood for dinner again?
That's the third time this week!'

If you are a baby pelican
and your mother makes this
face, it's time to panic

THE OWL

LATIN NAME: NOCTUA

WHERE IT ABIDES: ANYWHERE THAT THE LIGHT DOES NOT REACH, FOR THE OWL FEARS AND LOATHES THE SUN'S RAYS

STRENGTHS: ILLEGAL TO EAT

WEAKNESSES: DIFFICULT TO LOVE

VIRTUE: 2 ✳ **BEAUTY:** 1 ✳ **DANGER:** 2

The owl knows better than to go out during the day, for all the other birds hate the sight of its face and will attack it immediately. Or perhaps it is *because* the owl only flies by night that it is so reviled in the first place: after all, what honest creature would have any reason to skulk about in the shadows and gloom?

Indeed, it is so vile that the Bible takes care to specify exactly how owls should make us feel[1]:

> *"You are to detest these birds. They must not be eaten because they are detestable."*
> (LEVITICUS 11: 13–17)[1]

> 'I'm sensing a bit of enmity here, guys.'

---

1. Which, frankly, leaves very little room for ambiguity.

Fool and his owl, France, 15th century

onùnùs cuftodierit cuntatem; fruftra
at qui cuftodit eam.

Owls are unholy creatures: this one should not have been permitted to become a bishop. Thankfully, the situation is being addressed

THE CALADRIUS

LATIN NAME: CALADRIUS

WHERE IT ABIDES: ITS PRESENCE HAUNTS THE BEDROOMS OF THE GRAVELY ILL

STRENGTHS: GOOD SENSE OF FORESIGHT

WEAKNESSES: NOT AN ADEQUATE REPLACEMENT FOR PROFESSIONAL MEDICAL CARE

VIRTUE: 5 ✲ **BEAUTY**: 2 ✲ **DANGER**: 2

The caladrius bird is pure white; white as bone. It possesses a very peculiar skill, for it can take one look at a sick person and know immediately whether they will die. If the patient's condition is mortal, then the caladrius will turn its back on them. If the patient will live, however, then the caladrius bird faces them, and gazes upon them, and with its gaze draws out the sickness into itself and flies off, carrying the illness far away and leaving the patient well.

This is a very cryptic bird, and it can be difficult to remember what its various messages mean.

Please take some time to familiarise yourself with the following images so that if you encounter a caladrius, you will be aware of what it is trying to tell you.

**Caladrius bird looking away from you
You will die soon**

**CALADRIUS BIRD
LOOKING
TOWARD YOU:**
You will survive

**ONE CALADRIUS
BIRD IN EACH
DIRECTION:**
It's a surprise!

**CALADRIUS BIRD
FROWNING:**
He knows
you're faking

**CALADRIUS BIRD
KISSES YOU:**
Romance in your future

BENEVOLENT BIRDS

(And other miraculous creatures)

Perhaps the most famous worker of animal-related miracles is Saint Francis, who famously preached to a flock of birds (who were very impressed indeed) and convinced a hungry wolf to stop eating villagers and their sheep. But 500 years before him lived a saint whose connection with nature was just as powerful: Saint Cuthbert of Lindisfarne. In addition to being the patron saint of Northumbria, Cuthbert is remembered for his goodwill toward all living things and the many animals that came to his aid during his life.

Here are a few highlights from Cuthbert's extensive repertoire of miracles:

While Cuthbert and his companion were wandering in the hills, they grew very hungry and fatigued but were unable to find anything to eat

Cuthbert had built for his guests a small house with a thatched roof

Cuthbert recited all 150 psalms to the young lad, which helped about as much as expected, and their hunger persisted. Suddenly, an eagle flew up to the two wanderers and dropped a salmon before them. Before Cuthbert took any of the fish for himself, he instructed his companion to slice off a portion for the eagle as thanks for its kindness.

One day, several ravens began to steal straw from the roof to make their own nests.

Cuthbert told the birds off, saying that they were causing harm to his poor visitors, and the ravens flew off in shame. Later on, one of the ravens returned with a piece of pig's lard for Cuthbert, who accepted the apology.[1]

---

1. Logically, it seems that it would be difficult for a raven to acquire a piece of lard without stealing that, too, but Cuthbert wasn't one to pry.

On another long journey, Cuthbert found himself running out of food once again

While staying at a monastery, Cuthbert would go outside at night and not return until morning

He stumbled upon an empty shepherd's hut and decided to spend the night there, while his horse decided to snack on some straw from the roof.[2] As the horse pulled mouthfuls of straw out of the thatching, Cuthbert was shocked to see a linen cloth fall out, too, and inside the cloth was a warm loaf of bread and a piece of meat, which Cuthbert shared with his horse and both were revitalised.

A curious monk followed him one evening in secret and saw Cuthbert walking down to the beach, where he waded into the water up to his neck and stood there all night singing prayers. When Cuthbert walked back out onto the sand, two otters followed him. The otters used their fur to dry Cuthbert's feet and their breath to warm them, then scampered back into the ocean.[3]

---

2. Apparently it's okay when it's *other* people's roofs.
3. Several people, upon hearing this, asked whether the otters wouldn't also be wet after emerging from the ocean, making it hard for them to dry someone else off. There's a simple answer here: it's a miracle. Don't overthink it.

Plants can be weird little guys, too!

Italy, 15th century

A light snack, Netherlands, ca. 15th century

FISH

CREATURES THAT SWIM IN THE SEAS

F ish are the creatures that swim in the seas. There are numerous varieties of fish: some say as many as 144, though that may be hard to believe. It must be nice, in some ways, to be a fish, because they do very little and hardly possess any high level of thought. Most fish can be eaten, however, and we are very lucky for the fact because they would otherwise be useful for little else. They fill the seas in great abundance and scarcely protest when we pull them up on to land for supper, a true sign of benevolence among the aquatic species.

Some fish cannot be eaten, however. Either they don't taste right or they make themselves too much of an ordeal to catch and kill, and these are by and large the ones you'll need to look out for. These fish are bad news. Remember, then, next time you're reeling a fish up from

the depths that it could just as easily be *you* getting dragged *down*. Just like the devil waits for moments of weakness to entice you to sin, you may never know what sorts of monsters are lurking just below the surface waiting to strike.

THE FISH

LATIN NAME: PISCIS

WHERE IT ABIDES: YOU SHOULD ALREADY KNOW WHERE FISH LIVE

STRENGTHS: PLENTY OF THEM IN THE SEA

WEAKNESSES: POSSIBLY TOO DELICIOUS?

VIRTUE: 3 ✻ **BEAUTY:** 3 ✻ **DANGER:** 2

The fish is a creature that swims about in vast numbers in the depths of the ocean. Fish are known to be excellent parents: upon laying their eggs in an underwater nest, the mother leaves immediately and is never seen again. This may seem harsh, but nevertheless represents a marked improvement on how most human parents go about their job.

On Fridays, Christians are not allowed to eat meat, but they are allowed to eat seafood. Luckily for the Irish, it is rumoured that there lives in their country a type of goose called the barnacle goose, which hatches not from eggs but from barnacles and kelp in the sea. This classifies it as a type of fish, meaning it's fair game for Friday dinner.[1]

---

1. In 1215, Pope Innocent III outlawed the practice of eating barnacle geese on fast days. He admitted that while it *was* true that the geese hatched from barnacles, he still felt that they fell more into the bird category than the fish category.

'Yeah that's fine, they'll all be in the ocean anyway
so no one's really going to see them. I'll just create the bears
and stuff tomorrow and then call it a week'

THE WHALE

LATIN NAME: CETUS

WHERE IT ABIDES: ROAMING ACROSS THE WORLD'S OCEANS IN SEARCH OF SMALLER CREATURES TO SWALLOW UP

STRENGTHS: EXPERT IN CAMOUFLAGE, GREAT AT DROWNING THINGS

WEAKNESSES: DOESN'T LIKE BEING SET ON FIRE

VIRTUE: 2 ✳ **BEAUTY:** 1 ✳ **DANGER:** 4

The whale is a monster of the sea, and a very dangerous fish. It is said that the whale is so big, and its back so covered in seaweed and barnacles, that sailors mistake it for an island and sail up to it to drop their anchor. Because of its tremendous size and very thick skin, the whale doesn't even notice the sailors until they build a fire upon it to cook their food. Then, feeling the heat of the flames at last, the whale dives down to the depths of the ocean to cool itself off. In the process, the sailors and their ship are dragged down, too, and every one of them is drowned.

'Hey, God, so, I'm ready to give the whole prophet thing another go. Not for any particular reason, of course'

So next time you're out sailing and see a convenient island in the middle of the sea, maybe just double check?

The dangers of getting too close to whales are illustrated in the biblical story of Jonah. Jonah was a prophet who fancied a career change, so he tried to run away from God by getting on a boat and sailing far away. God, who tends to notice these things fairly quickly, sent a massive storm to block the boat's path. Feeling that he would rather die than have to go back to his job, Jonah allowed the sailors to toss him overboard, where he was immediately swallowed whole by a massive whale.

God left Jonah in the whale's stomach for three days and three nights, until he finally felt that Jonah was sufficiently sorry for his delinquency and told the whale to spit him back up. Thus, an important lesson was learned: be careful about double-crossing the Lord Himself, because He can always send a whale out to get you. Seriously, you'd be surprised where He can hide whales. It's no joke.

'Well, one of us is going to have to let him go'

THE EEL

ske-squyys y dymuniib is ye. 2lud yne is y'nlny y'yei be zondy alayn. but it fallyrh sittyme y'pe dymunnud's lylyrh lypo bru yo asinite of lynn y'berythzt. 2 y be mnup othyr peyous konys. 2lud uis cleppyd ynde for nlbut y'reunyrh porlis it y'qlbyche ttatter is cleppyd ynde.

LATIN NAME: ANGUILLA

WHERE IT ABIDES: JUST LIKE MONEY LIVES AT THE BANK, EELS LIVE AT THE RIVER BANK

STRENGTHS: A SOUND INVESTMENT, HARDER TO STEAL THAN GOLD

WEAKNESSES: MIGHT SLIP BETWEEN YOUR FINGERS IF YOU DON'T ACT FAST

VIRTUE: 3 ✳ **BEAUTY:** 2 ✳ **DANGER:** 2

The eel is a long and slender fish that winds through shallow water in serpentine motions. Some people say that eels are born directly out of river mud – no parents or anything, just mud. Perhaps it is because of this they are so slippery. Just like love, the tighter you grasp an eel, the more quickly it wriggles away.

Eels are an extremely common fish and are useful for all sorts of things. Not only do they make a lovely supper,[1] but many humble labourers in England pay their rent and other dues entirely with eels.[2] It may sound too good to be true, but you'd be surprised how far a few thousand bushels of eels can get you these days.

1. One surviving recipe from medieval France is for something called 'eels reversed'.
2. The full scale of the medieval eel economy remains hitherto unknown. However, it has been ascertained that in peak years, over half a million eels changed hands as a form of rent.

If it's good enough for a heron, it's good enough for me

**Note the two eel traps on the left: this house is basically paying for itself.
That's the power of the eel**

THE MERMAID

LATIN NAME: SERRA

WHERE IT ABIDES: HOPEFULLY NOWHERE NEAR YOU, SAILOR

STRENGTHS: VERY OUTGOING, LOVES TO CHAT

WEAKNESSES: BAD AT GIVING DIRECTIONS, STRUGGLES WITH TELLING THE TRUTH

VIRTUE: 2 ✻ **BEAUTY:** 5 ✻ **DANGER:** 4

The mermaid appears to be an astonishingly beautiful woman from the waist up, but her lower half is that of a fish, and though she can breathe air like a human, her true home is below the surface of the sea. These fish-women are wicked and vain and, above all, they are misandrists (and maybe even misanthropes altogether). They use their beauty and wiles to lure sailors to the edges of their ships, where they drag the poor souls below the water to their doom.

A mermaid is always a bad omen, for they appear before doomed ships, telling them that they are but a short distance from harbour when in truth not a single man aboard will ever see land again. It is not known whether mermaids are the cause of disaster or simply a sign of it, but this makes no difference to the fates of those who they encounter. If you should happen to encounter a mermaid, the best course of action is to cater to her vanity. You might tell her, for instance, that she has beautiful eyes and her scales are looking particularly ravishing this morning. This will not make the mermaid spare you your watery demise, but if you're really convincing, she might get it over with a bit quicker.

Female mermaids use their astonishing beauty to seduce sailors, while the less attractive mermen must rely on their skills in logic and rhetoric.

Maidmer, Germany, 13th century

NOT QUITE HUMAN BEINGS

Hybrid creatures appear all over medieval art, most frequently decorating the margins of manuscripts. While these figures – often a mishmash of human, animal and monstrous parts – were designed to entertain the reader, they also reflect a curious facet of medieval thought. In a world that was understood to be the product of intentional design, beings that did not conform to standards of external beauty and normality must surely be that way for a reason. And what could that reason be but to reflect an internal, moral deviance? A spiritual ugliness?

These beings were corruptions of normal human nature, ruled by lust, violence and other sins rather than by reason and morals. Their supposedly corrupted bodies, in conflict with God's design, were a physical embodiment of these defects. And in the context of a medieval manuscript, they stood in stark contrast to the prayers, lessons and richly illustrated biblical scenes that occupied the main pages.

Despite their unsympathetic origins, the creatures concocted by medieval illuminators are often amusing and even endearing. Looking at the various hybrid creatures on this page –not quite human, not quite beast –it's easy to imagine their artists thought so, too.

**Doing a little dance,
Flanders, 13th century**

Torment, France, 14th century

Worm getting drunk,
France, c. 1405

Doctor dog treating sick cat,
15th century

Useful creature, Flanders,
13th century

Armed and dangerous, England, 15ᵗʰ century

Merman, France, 15th century

THE CROCODILE

LATIN NAME: COCODRILLUS

WHERE IT ABIDES: LURKING BENEATH MUDDY WATER IN THE RIVER NILE

STRENGTHS: BUILT TO KILL, LOVES A BIT OF KILLING

WEAKNESSES: GUILT COMPLEX, VERY SELF-CRITICAL

VIRTUE: 2 ✳ **BEAUTY**: 1 ✳ **DANGER**: 4

The crocodile is a fearsome beast with skin like armour and teeth like sabres. It likes to lurk beneath the surface of the river in wait for unsuspecting prey, and its favourite prey of all is humans. It has been common knowledge for a long time that while a crocodile is eating its prey, it weeps, but never stops eating, shedding the tears of a sinner who knows that they will never be free from sin.[1] Many people are like this, failing to cease their wicked deeds, although in all fairness it's not easy to stop once you're tucking in to a good meal.

The only creature that can kill the crocodile is a small serpent called the hydrus. When it sees the crocodile sleeping, the hydrus slips inside its mouth and then eats its way out of the crocodile's belly, killing it.

The two main lessons here are:

1. Don't sin.
2. Sleep with your mouth closed.

---

1. Crocodiles, like many reptiles, do in fact have tear ducts. They cry to keep their eyes from drying out while above water, rather than as an expression of guilt – a crocodile's brain likely does not possess the relevant faculties to experience guilt. It has been shown, however, that crocodiles are able feel anxiety.

ft animal in nlo flumme qd dicit ydru in aqua ydr

'Just popping in for a second!'

THE SNAIL

LATIN NAME: COCHLEA

WHERE IT ABIDES: SNAILS ONLY APPEAR IN WET CONDITIONS, DWELLING BENEATH THE SEA OR POPPING UP FROM THE GROUND WHEN IT RAINS

STRENGTHS: SAVES MONEY ON RENT

WEAKNESSES: TERMINALLY LATE, JUST CAN'T KEEP UP

VIRTUE: 3 ✳ **BEAUTY**: 2 ✳ **DANGER**: 1

The snail is a very small, slimy creature that moves at an exceedingly slow pace, which allows it to prey most efficiently on leaves and fruit. It doesn't mind moving along at such a crawl because it usually doesn't have much going on, socially speaking. The snail carries its home upon its back wherever it goes, which is very convenient because an errant kick from a pedestrian could extend its evening commute by a fortnight.

Certain types of snail secrete a substance that can be turned into a beautiful dye in all shades of red and purple. However, garments made with this colour are very expensive because snails are rather small and it takes quite a few of them to just dye some stockings, never mind a robe or mantle. Therefore, anyone you see dressed in that unmistakable snail-y hue is sure to be a person of great importance and wealth.

A lesser known fact about snails is that they yearn for the freedom of the skies and love to feel the wind on their shells as they sail through the air

Snails have shells to protect themselves from predators, and large boyfriends to protect themselves from other kinds of predators

KNIGHTS VS SNAILS

It's not just rabbits who find themselves in all sorts of mischief on the pages of medieval manuscripts. Snails, too, often appear in uncharacteristically violent scenarios, squaring off with knights and soldiers. The mystery of what these snails and their battles represent has baffled historians even to this day.

Did they represent class struggle? Hatred for the French? Difficulties with garden pests? Did people just think snails were funny? We may never know what caused medieval illustrators to draw snail battles so many centuries ago, but we can enjoy the silly scenes that have been left behind.

**Remember:
Snails have built-in armour,
so don't try to fight one naked.
The snail will have the upper hand**

**Here's the proper way
to dress for a snail fight**

Attack on snail,
France,
15th century

No match for the killer snail,
we see that this knight has swiftly
surrendered and is praying for
mercy from his captor. The snail
seems to have gained the ability
to levitate at some point

'This is possibly more escargot than we are able to consume
in a single evening, but that's not going to stop us from trying, is it?'

SERPENTS

CREATURES THAT CRAWL ON THE GROUND

Serpents are all creatures covered in scales and slime. They creep and crawl about on their stomachs in the dirt, some say as punishment for tempting Eve with the forbidden fruit all those years ago. There is little to like about the serpents: most are filthy creatures with very little use to us and no shortage of danger. Most have cold blood and fangs that drip with potent venom which they do not hesitate to dispense. Don't go trying to make friends with any serpents: they are bad because God made them that way, and there's not much that can be done about that.

We can learn from their evils, though.

We can pray to never become like them, for they serve as a living reminder that there is truly horror on Earth. We can try to understand their wickedness so that it may be better avoided, and we can carry on hoping that we do not one day find ourselves crawling about in the dirt right next to them.

THE DRAGON

LATIN NAME: DRACO[1]

WHERE IT ABIDES: IN THE FURTHEST CORNERS OF THE EARTH, DEEP INSIDE CAVES WITHIN HILLS AND MOUNTAIN SIDES

STRENGTHS: FRIENDS IN LOW PLACES

WEAKNESSES: FORSAKEN BY ALL THAT IS GOOD AND HOLY

VIRTUE: 1 ✳ **BEAUTY:** 2 ✳ **DANGER:** 5

The dragon is the most enormous of all serpents, just as the devil is the greatest of all evils. It is a gargantuan winged beast, covered in scales that spits fire upon its victims. Just like the devil was once an angel, the dragon too may appear at first to be a creature of the Heavens, borne through the air on its massive, reptilian wings. But make no mistake: though it may have the power of flight, it belongs to the underbelly of the Earth, just as the devil does, and will do everything it can to bring innocent souls down to the depths of Hell with it.

---

1. The Vikings had many nicknames for the dragon. Among them are: hoard-warden, twilight-scather, hateful air-goer, plague-of-the-people, poison-foe.

'Really? With the dragon?'

'Do you mind?'

THE SNAKE

. Serpens.

LATIN NAME: SERPENS

WHERE IT ABIDES: SNAKES, UNFORTUNATELY, ARE ALL OVER THE PLACE

STRENGTHS: FEMININE WILES, EXCELLENT SALESMANSHIP

WEAKNESSES: NO ARMS IS PRETTY EMBARRASSING

VIRTUE: 1 ✳ **BEAUTY:** 2 ✳ **DANGER:** 3

The snake is a wicked serpent that is covered in slime and causes agonising death with its venomous bite. The snake is a creature that lives very close to the ground – that is, close to Hell – for it has not arms nor legs, but rather slithers around in the dirt on its belly.

Many poets and scholars have warned us that women are just like snakes. Although women have legs and do not slither around on their bellies (that we are aware of) it is well known that women, like snakes, are naturally inclined to sin and betrayal. Was it not Eve who committed the first sin? If it were not for women, we would still be hanging out naked in the Gar-den of Eden making friends with the animals and eating figs for every meal. Next time your wife starts getting a bit uppity, make sure you remind her whose gender it was ruined that.

If women aren't just like snakes, then why do they look so similar?

Helpful advice: before you take a sip from your goblet, have a look to make sure there's wine inside it rather than a snake. You wouldn't want to drink a snake

THE SALAMANDER

LATIN NAME: SALAMANDRA

WHERE IT ABIDES: WHEREVER A FIRE IS BURNING, A SALAMANDER WILL BE DRAWN TO THE SCENE

STRENGTHS: HOT BODY

WEAKNESSES: STAGGERING HEATING BILLS

VIRTUE: 3 ✳ **BEAUTY:** 2 ✳ **DANGER:** 2

The salamander is perhaps the most deadly of all serpents, not just because of the strength of its venom but also because it can kill great numbers in a single blow, for all that it touches becomes infected with a deadly toxin. If a salamander crawls through the branches of a fruit tree, all those who eat the fruit will drop dead immediately.

Salamanders also have the marvellous property of being impervious to fire. In fact, they seek out the flames and love to sit within them. A salamander's body is so cold that it actually extinguishes fires and so often when a blacksmith's forge refuses to light, he looks inside his furnace for the culprit, which is usually an errant little salamander.

Some say that the salamander represents the virtuous soul, because it endures great hardship without coming to harm like the three boys in the Bible saved by an angel from the fiery furnace. Others say that the salamander represents the sinner, because it can burn eternally without being consumed, like a soul in Hell. It's hard to say which is true, but it's still pretty neat.

Egregious abuse of the 'I licked it so it's mine' rule

King Nebuchadnezzar (left) trying to deflect the blame for chucking three kids into a furnace. Daniel (centre) letting us know who the real culprit is

This salamander might not resemble a serpent per se, but 'serpent' is just as much a state of mind as anything else

THE BASILISK

LATIN NAME: REGULUS

WHERE IT ABIDES: IN DARK CAVES OR FOUL BURROWS BENEATH THE GROUND, WHICH ARE SO POLLUTED BY ITS POISON THAT NO OTHER CREATURE WILL COME NEAR

STRENGTHS: BICULTURAL UPBRINGING, WELL-RESPECTED COMMUNITY LEADER

WEAKNESSES: WEASELS, FERRETS, MINK, STOATS

VIRTUE: 1 ✸ **BEAUTY:** 1 ✸ **DANGER:** 5

The basilisk is a frightening creature with the head and body of a rooster but the tail of a serpent. It is said to be the unholy offspring of a chicken and a snake, and though it is hardly bigger than a chicken, the basilisk breathes a poison so potent that any living thing near by dies immediately.

The basilisk's Latin name, *Regulus*, means 'king'. This is on account of the fact that all the other serpents regard the basilisk as their ruler and dare not attack it. But not because they're scared of it or anything. Basilisks are just very charismatic and likeable.

It is common knowledge that the only creature capable of killing a basilisk is a weasel, so if a basilisk has taken up residence on your land, you need only track down a weasel, stuff it in a bag, take it to the basilisk's lair, and throw it in: the weasel handles the rest.

Then, instead of a basilisk, your property will be home to a vicious carnivorous beast who presumably didn't enjoy being kidnapped and chucked in the direction of a noxious, cave-dwelling rooster-snake. Once you sort out that situation, you're in the clear. Good luck!

'I hope he has his daddy's eyes and his mummy's ability
to kill grown men with a single bite'

'Look, I'm not happy about this either'

THE FROG

LATIN NAME: RANA

WHERE IT ABIDES: IN THE LEAVES, MUD AND DIRT, WHERE IT BLENDS RIGHT IN

STRENGTHS: FEW AND FAR BETWEEN

WEAKNESSES: NOT AS GROSS AS IT COULD HAVE BEEN

VIRTUE: 1 ✻ **BEAUTY**: 1 ✻ **DANGER**: 5

The frog is a very foul and ugly little thing. Not much is known of the lives and habits of frogs, probably because few people care enough to find out. Some say that frogs eat only dirt, and some even say that they are born spontaneously out of the dirt. Either way, they are creatures of the dirt.

A frog is a bad omen, for it symbolises poison and false speech. Frogs were one of the plagues sent to the Pharaoh in the book of Exodus, and are said to jump from the mouths of the dragon, the beast and the false prophet who bring about the apocalypse in Revelations. Not a good track record.

'What an evil-looking creature'

'Look, guys, I'm a false prophecy!'

Crazy frog, France, 13th century

THE AMPHISBAENA

LATIN NAME: AMPHISBAENA

WHERE IT ABIDES: WITH ITS OTHER HALF

STRENGTHS: NEVER GETS LONELY

WEAKNESSES: A LITTLE BIT TOO ATTACHED

VIRTUE: 2 ✳ **BEAUTY**: 2 ✳ **DANGER**: 3

The amphisbaena is a snake with two heads, one on either end of its body, and each is as venomous as the other. This curious creature can move whichever way it pleases, and so is able to strike out without warning in any direction.

It is said that the amphisbaena has all sorts of magical properties. For instance, rumour has it that eating the flesh of this serpent will make you irresistible to the opposite sex, and that anyone who slays the amphisbaena by moonlight will attain special powers, so long as the person is of pure heart and mind.[1] Another source says that women wishing to have a safe pregnancy need only wear a live amphisbaena around their necks and then their baby will be carried and delivered without complication.[2]

---

1. But not so pure that they would have any issue with slaying an innocent snake for their own personal benefit, I suppose.
2. It's unclear how well the amphisbaena will respond to this.

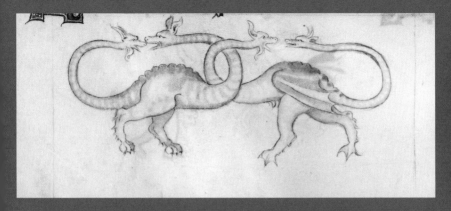

If two pregnant amphisbaenae loop around each other's necks,
they're guaranteed to both have lots of healthy little snake babies

'Ignore him – he's just jealous that he was born on the wrong side of the snake'

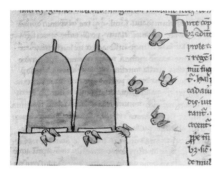

Normal bats, England, 13th century

Sweet little peanuts, flying off to their well-endowed hive. That's what bees are. France, 13th century

Boar wearing pants, France, 14th century

Possibly the cutest ever rendition of a bat, England, 13th century

Fish man, Persia, 16ᵗʰ century

Cat fish, Persia, 16ᵗʰ century

IN THE END

Just as the world was created,
there are those who believe it will eventually end.

In the end, everything will be destroyed. That much, most of
us agree on. As for *how* the world will end, though, hypotheses
vary. But a long time ago, one man, a prophet, said that he had
heard all about it straight from the source. God Himself sent
this prophet visions of the end, and he wrote them all down
in a book: the story of the apocalypse yet to come.
Would you like to know what will happen?
Well, fire will rain down from the sky, for starters.

You'll see four horsemen summoned to sow death and
destruction across all of the Earth:

The first

will come on a white horse
and carry a bow, bringing
conquest with him.

The second

will come on a red horse
and carry a sword,
bringing war with him.

The third

will come on a black horse
and carry scales, bringing
famine with him.

The last horseman

will ride out of the mouth of
Hell on a pale horse. All of Hell
will follow behind him, for this
horseman is named Death.

From the ground and the sea will rise a seven-headed dragon,
a seven-headed beast and other unsavoury types walking around,
spewing blasphemy, false prophecies and frogs out of their lying mouths.
Those who believe the false prophecies and swear loyalty to these
creatures will be marked on their foreheads with the sign of the Beast.

A lot more happens, but most of it amounts to this:
chaos, death and destruction for the people of the Earth.

Of course, God won't destroy *all* of His creation. That would be excessive.
A few will be saved, but only if they stay faithful to Him – so the story goes, at
least. For all the armies of Heaven will descend upon the Earth to fight the
forces of evil.

If you stick around until the end, things should start to look up. Don't listen to the false prophets and beasts, okay? Don't follow the sinners. None of them make it out of this story. They get sent right back to where they came from.

And after that? When the Earth has been reduced to smoking rubble, and only the good people are left? That's the best part: God Himself will return to the Earth, and this time He won't leave. He'll fix everything, and we will all be healed, and the world will be made into Paradise again, just as it was before everything went wrong.

Makes you wonder why we had to go through so much just to get back to where we started in the first place, doesn't it?

That's one for another day, though.

CREDITS

Library, Yates Thompson 28, fol. 44r

p. 154 London, British Library, Yates Thompson 29, fol. 14r

p. 154 London, British Library, Yates Thompson 30, fol. 24r

p. 155 Philadelphia, UPenn, Oversize LJS 419, fol. 42r

p. 155 Philadelphia, UPenn, Oversize LJS 419, fol. 77r

p. 165 Bosch, Hieronymus. The Garden of Earthly Delights. 1490-150, Prado Museum, Madrid.

p. 157 Los Angeles, J. Paul Getty Museum, MS 100, fol. 48v

p.159 London, British Library, Add. 11639, fol. 518v

p. 160 Los Angeles, J. Paul Getty Museum, Ms. Ludwig XIII 5, v1, fol. 35

p. 161 Los Angeles, J. Paul Getty Museum, MS Ludwig XV 3 , fol. 89v

p. 161 Darmstadt, University Library, Hs 2505, fol. 61r"

p. 162 Paris, National Library of France, Français 145, fol. 7v

p. 163 London, British Library, Harley 3954, fol. 31v

p. 164 London, British Library, Royal 13 B. VIII, fol. 9

p. 164 London, British Library, Add. 42130, fol. 181

p. 165 London, British Library, Add. 18852, fol. 102

p. 165 Cleveland, Cleveland Museum of Art, 1964.4, fol.

193r

p. 166 London, British Library, Harley 5648, fol. 142v

p. 167 Baltimore, Walters Art Museum, W.37, fol. 190v

p. 168 Los Angeles, J. Paul Getty Museum, MS Ludwig IX 5, fol. 14v

p. 168 Cleveland, Cleveland Museum of Art, 1964.4, fol. 168r

p. 168 Edinburgh, University Library, Db. 3.20, fol. 25v

p. 168 Baltimore, Walters Art Museum, W.37, fol. 187v

p. 169 Oxford, Bodleian Library, MS Bodl. 764, fol. 51r

p. 170 Oxford, Bodleian Library, MS Douce 337, fol. 11v

p. 171 London, British Library, Royal 12 F. XIII, fol. 24

p. 172 London, British Library, Harley 4751, fol. 62v

p. 173 London, British Library, Stowe 17, fol. 185

p. 174 Los Angeles, J. Paul Getty Museum, MS Ludwig IX 16, fol. 60

p. 174 Los Angeles, J. Paul Getty Museum, MS Ludwig XV 1, fol. 47v

p. 175 Baltimore, Walters Art Museum, W.90, fol. 39r

p. 175 London, British Library, Yates Thompson 19, fol. 65r

p. 176 Paris, National Library of France, Velins-518

p. 176 London, British

Library, Add 49622, fol. 162v, 193v

p . 176 Los Angeles, J. Paul Getty Museum, MS 124, fol. 32

p. 177 Los Angeles, J. Paul Getty Museum, Ms. 77

p. 179 Los Angeles, J. Paul Getty Museum, MS Ludwig IX 5, fol. 104v

p. 179 Los Angeles, J. Paul Getty Museum, MS 5, fol. 27v

p. 180 London, British Library,Burney 169, fol. 14

p. 180 London, British Library, Harley 2830, fol. 7

p. 181 Los Angeles, J. Paul Getty Museum, MS 33, fol. 103

p. 182 Los Angeles, J. Paul Getty Museum, MS 63, fol. 3

p. 182 London, British Library, King's 9, fol. 30v

p. 183 Los Angeles, J. Paul Getty Museum, MS 100, fol. 58

p. 184 London, British Library, Royal 2 B. VII, fol. 117

p. 184 Los Angeles, J. Paul Getty Museum, MS 33, fol. 212v

p. 184 Los Angeles, J. Paul Getty Museum, MS Ludwig XV 3, fol. 95v

p. 185 New Haven, Yale Center for British Art, Folio C 2014 4, fol. 18v

p. 186 London, British Library, Royal 2 B. VII, fol. 187v

p. 186 Los Angeles, J. Paul Getty Museum, MS 100, fol. 54v

p. 187 Zürich, Central

Library, Ms Rh hist 161, page 184

p. 188 Paris, National Library of France, Latin 8878, fol. 184v

p. 188 Paris, National Library of France, Latin 1226(1), fol. 44v

p. 189 Los Angeles, J. Paul Getty Museum, MS 100, fol. 58v

p. 190 London, British Library, Royal 2 B. VII, fol. 138v

p. 190 Los Angeles, J. Paul Getty Museum, MS 138, fol. 94

p. 191 London, British Library, Add. 36684, fol. 31r

p. 191 Paris, National Library of France, Latin 6838B , fol. 29v

p. 191 London, British Library, Harley 3244, fol. 55v

p. 192 Tehran, The National Library and Archives of Iran. Retrieved from the Library of Congress.

p. 192 Tehran, The National Library and Archives of Iran. Retrieved from the Library of Congress.

p. 193 London, British Library, Add. 17333, fol. 10v

p. 194 London, British Library, Royal 19 B. XV, fol. 9v-10v

p. 195 London, British Library, Royal 19 B. XV, fol. 30v

p. 196 London, British Library, Add. 17333, fol. 43

p. 196 London, British Library, Royal 15 D. II, fol. 117v

ACKNOWLEDGEMENTS

Weird Medieval Guys owes its existence to every real-life weird medieval guy who put pen to parchment and created the works you see here. Therefore, I would like to extend my thanks to everyone who lived roughly between the 5th and the 15th centuries AD, and especially Christine de Pizan, Boccaccio, Edward, 2nd Duke of York, Saint Cuthbert, William the Conqueror for putting together the Domesday book but not for what he did to the Anglo-Saxons, and Hieronymus Bosch.

The images in this book were found among the thousands of medieval manuscripts that have been digitised and published online. The people and institutions who have spent years working to make these books accessible to the world are owed my endless gratitude.

I would like to express my thanks to my mom for her uncanny knack for brainstorming, my dad for his scones, and both my parents for their infinite wisdom, patience and love. To my entire family, my wonderful friends, and everyone else who I did not text back while writing this book, I'm sorry about that and forever grateful for your nevertheless ceaseless support and kindness throughout the past year. In particular I am so very grateful to my partner Daniel, without whom I probably would have exploded.

Thanks to my agent Tom Killingbeck, who is a wizard, and everyone at Square Peg, who are all magicians, for conjuring this book into existence by some powers beyond my understanding.

And, most importantly, thanks to the 700,000 or so of you (and counting!) that have followed Weird Medieval Guys and made running the account such a positive experience with your kind words and enthusiasm.

ABOUT THE
AUTHOR

One of the internet's foremost culture vultures,
Olivia Swarthout prowls the web for little-seen snippets
of medieval art and life to share with the world via the
Weird Medieval Guys Twitter and Instagram accounts.
Described by her mother as having 'a knack for curation'
she uses her platform to shine a light on the so-called
'Dark Ages' and bring people closer to the distant past.

Born in the Rocky Mountains of Montana, USA,
Olivia's enduring love of cowboy boots and the great
outdoors has survived many years of living in Berlin,
Glasgow and London, where she currently resides
and works.